Pluralism in Software Engineering:
Turing Award Winner Peter Naur Explains

Edgar G. DAYLIGHT

This transcript has been edited
by Edgar G. Daylight, Kurt De Grave, and Peter Naur.

LONELY SCHOLAR™
SCIENTIFIC BOOKS

Published by Lonely Scholar bvba
Sint-Lambertusstraat 3
3001 Heverlee
Belgium
editor@lonelyscholar.com
http://www.lonelyscholar.com

D/2011/12.695/1
ISBN 978-94-9138-600-8
ISSN 2034-5976
NUR 980, 732

Praise for
Pluralism in Software Engineering:
Turing Award Winner Peter Naur Explains

"What an absolutely cool guy!"

— Dennis Shasha
New York University

"[F]ascinating... the interview is a very worthwhile contribution to documenting the history of the field, and will be of strong interest both to computer scientists and to professional historians"

— Robert Harper
Carnegie Mellon University

Contents

Biography

Peter Naur was born in 1928 in Frederiksberg, Denmark. He graduated from Copenhagen University in astronomy in 1949 and was a research student at King's College, Cambridge in 1950–51 where he programmed the EDSAC in order to solve an astronomical problem. After a year's stay in the USA and a brief return to Cambridge, Naur spent the rest of the 1950s in Copenhagen. In 1957 he received his PhD in astronomy and in 1959 he joined the staff of Regnecentralen, specializing in high-level programming languages. He became heavily involved in the design and implementation of ALGOL60 and organized the ALGOL Bulletin. From 1969 until his retirement in 1999 he was professor at the Copenhagen University Institute of Datalogy. Since the mid-1990s until this day, Naur actively studies and writes about psychology and in particular about how human life is like at the neural level of the nervous system. He has received several awards, including the Computer Pioneer Award of the IEEE Computer Society in 1986 and the ACM Turing Award in 2005.

Preface

April 5th, 2011 — it was a moderately warm spring day in Copenhagen. I was sitting on a bench in Gentofte, one of Copenhagen's wealthy suburbs. My hotel was only two kilometers away and, more importantly, only 100 meters parted me from my final destination, an old-looking house which I had already walked by a couple of times earlier during the morning. The house reminded me of a fairy tale and its surrounding garden gave me the impression that the house was deserted.

Sitting on the bench, I waited for my watch to give the go-ahead signal. I would start walking at 1:57 pm and knock on the house's front door at 2:00 pm. Even though I had already interviewed prominent researchers before, I nervously wondered how Peter Naur would be like in person. I had exchanged letters with him and I had eagerly studied his writings during the previous 18 months. Nevertheless, I definitely was a little bit anxious.

I knocked on the door. Some 10 seconds later, a tall and gentle-looking man welcomed me. He was physically in great shape, looking 20 years younger than I had anticipated. His welcoming gesture comforted me immediately. It was as if we were already acquainted. His living room strengthened the impression I had obtained from the outside: it was a mess. Books, papers, paintings, and some musical instruments were laying all over the place. The computer and the printer in the corner were from the 1990s and thus, from my standpoint, antique. The kitchen was absolutely... well, I have promised Naur I wouldn't describe his kitchen in writing.

The mess was an absolute delight to my eyes. Here lives an authentic lonely scholar, a rare species that reads and writes with the sole purpose to understand. The mess not only put my anxiety aside, it also visually re-confirmed my initial expectations: I felt then that the discussion was going to be well worth our time. In fact, one afternoon with Naur was not enough; I returned some 5 weeks later to continue the discussion.

The result is an extensive dialogue with the 2005 Turing Award winner Peter Naur, a dialogue which encompasses several topics. Throughout his career, Naur has jumped from one discipline to another — e.g. from compiler writing to philosophy, or from psychology on problem solving to structured programming (and back again). The dialogue reflects this diversity. It is semi-structured in that I have only tried to chronologically order Naur's accomplishments. On several occasions, side alleys are entered, only to later return to the main topic with a more prepared mindset.

Three parts constitute this booklet. Part I was conducted on the 5th of April, 2011. Parts II and III were conducted some weeks later, on the 14th and 17th of May, respectively. Part I should be of interest to most readers. Part II delves into the details of philosophy, program development, and Dijkstra's "pleasantness problem". Part III elaborates on Naur's recent research on psychology and helps the computer programmer comprehend, with hindsight, Parts I and II with much greater precision. Vice versa, Parts I and II aid the philosopher and psychologist in grasping Naur's preparatory work which led to his latest accomplishments in neurology.

This booklet has been written with two main objectives in mind: (i) sharing with the open-minded reader what I have learned during the spring of 2011, and (ii) presenting an extensive overview of Naur's research contributions, supplemented with several bibliographical references to his original writings.

The Backus-Naur Form is only mentioned in passing, because I believe it are Naur's post-**ALGOL** contributions which have yet to receive the full attention they deserve.

I hope this booklet will incite the reader's curiosity, regardless of whether his or her interest lies in astronomy, computer programming, philosophy, or psychology.

Edgar G. Daylight, September 2011, Leuven, Belgium.

Part I

1. Early Years

Daylight: Peter Naur, you were born in Frederiksberg, Denmark in 1928.

Naur: Yes, Frederiksberg is a part of Copenhagen really. It's not very far from here.

D: Did you have siblings?

N: I had one sister and one brother, five years and two years older than me.

D: As a child, did you enjoy playing football?

N: No, not really. I liked to play Meccano until I got caught in astronomy. Those were two very different hobbies. The switch in interest happened when I changed schools. I must have been 11 or 12 years old. The geography teacher had suggested that we should watch the stars and the Big Dipper in particular. I did this and made several drawings because I thought it was an excellent exercise. It turned out that I was the only one in the class who had done a sensible job. This fired my interest in astronomy. For years thereafter, I was just very keen on understanding astronomy.

After a few years, I got interested in the computation of orbits of newly discovered comets and planets. It was an activity that was well supported by the observatory of Copenhagen. I got very much help from the people there. One of their staff members, Jens P. Møller, helped and supported me with my computations. I got access to their hand-driven calculating machines. In a few years, I understood all of this and did useful work in astronomy, which was published. I also got a lot of support from my parents. That was how it all started.

D: During the second world war you learned English from the school books written by the Danish linguist Otto Jespersen. Were you at that time already intrigued by Jespersen's research on linguistics?

N: No, no. By that time I had become very interested in modern physics, including the works of Einstein and Bohr. I read about such things in the semi-popular literature: James Jeans's books on astronomy and Eddington's books, etc.

D: Was your interest in physics related to the fact that you wanted to specialize in astronomy, or were you reading these books because you wanted to obtain a general understanding?

N: It's hard to say. But I was definitely keen on astronomy. Of course, all this physics had a lot to do with astronomy. This was the time when it was discovered how the energy of the sun comes out by atomic processes. That is atomic theory. So things were completely wielded together. In later years I worked on the interior of stars. When I got to America I computed models of the sun. It was published at that time, in 1952/53.

D: Did you during your school years also become acquainted with the works of some philosophers, such as Hume, Locke, and Kant? I am asking this because you mentioned to me in private correspondence that you had read Harald Hoffding's *Den nyere filosofis historie*, 1894.

N: You see, I always wanted to understand everything. I liked nothing better than the public library. I would browse through the books and ask myself what is psychology about.

D: So it wasn't just astronomy?

N: No not at all. But I got much further in astronomy because I was specializing in that.

D: Wasn't that difficult for you? On the one hand, doing that as a child must have been fun, you had lots of time to dig into these books. On the other hand, you were probably surrounded by children who had other interests, like playing football. Did you sense any difficulty?

N: Not a difficulty really. But I felt quite clearly that I was to some extent exceptional in my striving to understand science. The school work I found very easy, including the languages such as English and German. I started reading astronomy in German. The texts on computations of orbits was in German. So I knew more German before I started reading English.

D: You were not discouraged in any way to work on scientific problems in your teens?

N: No, no. I felt perfectly happy.

2. Cambridge: 1950–51

D: You went to King's College in Cambridge between October 1950 and June 1951.

N: That was after I had finished my degree in Copenhagen.

D: Could you elaborate a bit on the kind of work you did in Cambridge, compared to your work in Copenhagen? You worked on astronomy in both places, didn't you?

N: By 1950 it was already well known that Cambridge had the EDSAC computer. I had this double bill. I was working on astronomy and also on automatic computing. They had developed a technique for photometry with electronic means. That never got off the ground because the weather was so bad in Cambridge. Therefore, at a certain stage, I switched completely to programming and computation. I was also well prepared for this kind of work thanks to the computational work that I had done at the observatory in Copenhagen. I knew the techniques by hand, how to do these calculations such as integrating differential equations of motions of a small planet. I had been doing this for hundreds of hours in Copenhagen. So I was quite ready to prepare these computations for the EDSAC.

D: Did you keep a diary? Did you note down how you were progressing in your research on astronomy?

N: Well, I do have a skeleton of a diary. I can't remember when I started this. But I have been doing this for years. It has one page for every year. [Naur shows his notebook.] Here I started a computation on this comet and here I had a discussion about a specific topic, etc.

D: At a later age, when you were working on your PhD, did you extensively write down your ideas on paper in a form of a diary?

N: No, not like that. I do remember during my trip to the USA which was in 1952–53, when traveling around and visiting computing centers, that I started to write down my findings — I made a report on computers in the USA as I had perceived them. That report [32] is in Danish and was my way of formulating my experience. The most important part of it was the lesson from Cambridge, how they had organized their programming, the initial orders of Wheeler. His work on transforming the external form into the internal form was a very flexible and simple approach really. I immediately rearranged it so that it would suit our DASK machine that was being built in Copenhagen and which I believe was finished around 1957.

The DASK machine was inspired by the the design and electronics of the Stockholm machine, called the BESK, which was an excellent electronic device: high speed, very good design. But the programming style in Stockholm was very primitive and inconvenient. So I had the chance to contribute a much better system for the machine language of the DASK. This work led straight on to our later research on compilers for ALGOL [ALGOrithmic Language].

D: You mentioned Wheeler, but there were also Hartree, Wilkes, and Gill at Cambridge. How would you describe these people? Did some of them impress you? Did you know some better than others?

N: It was simply that I had gotten the chance to work on the EDSAC in Cambridge, it is not that I got to know any of those people personally. I got a table and the book *Report on the Preparation of Programs for the EDSAC and the Use of the Library of Subroutines* [70] and that was about it. That book contains a library of subroutines for the EDSAC and was also published in America a few years later. It was the source of insight which I could immediately use to start programming for my particular astronomical problem.

D: That was your only source? During the 1940s you had already worked on manual computations. You already knew how to do the numerical mathematics.

N: I was completely familiar with the technique of computation: developing numbers step by step according to a particular algorithm. That was completely by hand. It was just a matter of putting it on the EDSAC machine. My background as an astronomer was essential in this, as I've described in [44].

D: Did some of these people at Cambridge speak to you about Alan Turing? Did you meet Turing?

N: I never met Turing. I have a sort of a feeling that there was some antagonism between the Cambridge group and Turing's group at the National Physical Laboratory. How that was, I've never been able to understand. I have a feeling that they were not able to get on particularly well. I'm not sure whether Wilkes got on well with Turing or understood him too well.

D: It's not that they stressed Turing's 1936 paper [76] to you while you were at Cambridge?

N: No, no. The relation between Turing's work and the EDSAC I did not realize at that time at all. I'm not sure there was any relation because I think what Wilkes took over was the American work from von Neumann, Mauchley, and others. I'm sure Wilkes attended their course in Philadelphia on the UNIVAC. That's not directly derived from Turing, I'm quite sure about that. The American style was also in large part due to Atanasoff. It's explained in Randell's excellent account on *The Origins of Digital Computers: Selected Papers* [69]. Atanasoff invented so many things. His computer was automatic, binary, electronic, but it didn't do programming. [Pause] Turing's universal machine is of course a programmed computer. How exactly von Neumann got into that, I don't know.

D: Did you have a roommate at Cambridge? Did you have a lot of contact with other students?

N: I had an excellent relation with Peter Remnant, a Canadian research student of philosophy who later became professor of philosophy at Vancouver. I lived in a hostel, across the street from King's College. There were 20 or 30 students there and one kitchen. That's where I got into contact with Peter Remnant and also one physicist, Oliver Penrose, who is now professor in Edinburgh.

D: Is that the famous Penrose?

N: It's the brother of Roger Penrose. Oliver is a physicist and we were very friendly. I've seen him many times after my year in Cambridge. Nowadays I often have correspondence with him and discuss problems which we think are interesting.

D: About Peter Remnant, you mentioned to me in private correspondence that you talked to him regularly about a variety of subjects, including the work of Ryle, Wittgenstein, Russell, Peirce, and Quine. Can you elaborate on this?

N: We had our society of two for the discussion of meaningless questions. That was Remnant's idea, inspired by Kant who wrote somewhere that the man who asks a meaningless question and the other man tries to answer it, that is like one man milking a he-goat and the other man holding a sieve to catch the milk. Remnant was a real philosopher; he was five years older than me.

D: Did you read Wittgenstein in Cambridge?

N: At that time I was not much aware of Wittgenstein, not really.

D: Ryle?

N: He was one that Peter Remnant would have mentioned as a very prominent modern-day English philosopher. I didn't read Ryle's book *The Concept of Mind* until much later. That of course is an interesting book because so many people find it so very hard to understand or to grasp. Ryle criticized Descartes's idea of a soul in the body, or what he called the ghost in the machine. I realized decades later that he was 60 years late in that because William James [21] had already made that very clear in 1890. Ryle was not into James's work at all. He was strangely ambivalent about the subject of his book; it is not clear whether it was psychology or behavioralism. In this way, I found his book to be very unclear really.

D: Remnant and you probably talked about Bertrand Russell's work.

N: We talked about it. I remember that was just when Russell had published *History of Western Philosophy*. I recall Remnant quoting his teacher, professor C.D. Broad if I'm not mistaken, by referring to Russell's new book as "that absurd book".

D: Remnant was also the one who mentioned William James's book *The Principles of Psychology* [21] to you.

N: I would say that was the most striking advice he gave me. I didn't act on it at all at that time. But that was the source and it took some twenty years before I really got down to it. But he understood James's work perfectly.

D: In your recollections you wrote that Easter 1951 was an important moment for you [44]. The **EDSAC** was closed down so you were not able to run your program on the machine.

N: That's right. I had just revised my astronomical program so it was ready to be run on the machine. But since that was not possible, all I could do was sit down and look at my program carefully, trying to find the mistakes by hand. The result is that the day after the break holiday it all worked beautifully.

D: I do wonder, what were the other people in Cambridge doing during Easter? They weren't able to work on the machine either. Didn't they check their programs similarly to the way you did?

N: I don't know what they were doing. I didn't have close contact with them. We could come and go at the laboratory, just like that.

D: You have written that

> No one [in Cambridge] had any idea of how to analyse what went wrong in his program. [44, p.417]

N: The people at Cambridge had a particular prime-number test, a complicated program that was used to test the machine. It tested whether the machine was in a happy state or not. Those words you just quoted are Wilkes's which he sent to me around 1980, after I had sent him a draft version of my recollections [44]. No one knew how to analyze a program. Nowadays, I would cut it down section-wise, but nobody tried to do that.

D: So you were looking at the program text?

N: No no, it was just a tape with a machine. A tape with a handful of other tapes, auxiliary tapes for the machine. If you wanted to check whether the store was in a good state, you'd put in a particular tape and you could adjust the pulse frequency somewhere in the panel. They were all paper tapes.

D: When the EDSAC was shut down, you were looking at your paper tape. You didn't have the luxury at that moment to go to the machine and run your paper tape. Did your English colleagues have more of a tendency to go to the machine and operate it?

N: I couldn't tell for sure. But, of course, the group there was very much oriented to helping people find their mistakes. They had a whole family of auxiliary programs overlooking what happened, these programs could modify what happened. For example, instead of just executing the code, they would have an auxiliary program run at the same time which would take the instructions one by one. Besides executing these instructions, useful information would be printed out for each of these instructions as well. In this way you could then check whether your expectations with regards to execution were met. Another technique was to survey one particular storage cell. Every time something happened to that cell, you would be told what. These were the techniques that were developed there. I found Cambridge to be an excellent school of how to eliminate programming mistakes. All the business about library subroutines was just the same; that you should use as much as possible things that had already been checked out.

D: In Cambridge you were programming the **EDSAC** in order to solve an astronomical problem. It is clear from what we have been discussing that you had a strong urge to understand science and, in particular, to further the state of the art in astronomy. But were you also carefully planning your career at that time? Were you pursuing an academic career?

N: I already had a degree finished from Copenhagen. The next natural step would have been a doctorate. I only realized much later that I could have used my **EDSAC** program as the central topic of my PhD thesis. Instead, it was just published in a paper. I accomplished my actual doctorate thesis five years later. Though it was also based on my work with the **EDSAC**, it had a lot more results with regards to astronomical observations and positions.

3. From Astronomy to ALGOL

D: Did you, during the early 1950s, delve more into the work of Einstein?

N: Not really. I continued with astronomy after leaving Cambridge. I taught astronomy in Copenhagen for a while and then worked at the observatory in Copenhagen. Later, I moved into the new observatory which was being built in the middle of Sjaelland in Denmark, where I continued working on things which I had observed during my stay in the USA (1952–53).

D: What did you do during your stay in the USA?

N: Besides looking into American computers, I continued my work on astronomy. For instance, I made observations from the McDonald observatory in Texas. That was in cooperation with Bengt Strömgren. He was a very outstanding Danish astronomer and I owe him much gratitude. He became director of the Yerkes observatory in Wisconsin. I spent a month with him at the top of the mountains in Texas and observed the magnitudes and colors of a certain selection of stars. He had a particular program for which this was useful. I also computed models of the interior of the sun: how the temperature and pressure increases when you go into the sun, and how the state is such that there will be an energy production from nuclear processes. That was all in the USA. Pure astronomy with lots of calculations.

I also spent a summer in the Watson Lab in Manhattan, New York. The computing machines there were more primitive than the **EDSAC**. They were IBM punch-card machines: the 602A electromechanical calculator and the 604 electronic calculator. That was for working on the structure of stars, integrating differential equations.

D: The reason I mentioned Einstein again is because you wrote in your letter to me that you had a copy of Einstein's *The meaning of relativity*, dated 17 June 1950. You also wrote an obituary of Einstein [34] and you had a copy of his *Out of my later years* from around that time.

N: Yes, I wrote his obituary which shows that I was very well aware of his activities.

D: You also wrote that you had become acquainted with the following authors by the mentioned dates:

- Whitehead's *Adventures of Ideas*, by 31 January 1951.
- Gallie's *Peirce and Pragmatism*, by 1952.
- Britton's *John Stuart Mill*, by 25 January 1957.
- Russell's *Mysticism and Logic,* by 25 January 1957.

N: That were Pelican books which I happened to pick up. I would usually read it and get an impression of what was happening there.

D: Did you discuss these books with any of your colleagues in astronomy?

N: It was Peter Remnant, no one in Danish astronomy.

D: In 1957 you had Russell's *Mysticism and Logic*. Do you recall whether you also bought this book, or did you borrow it?

N: Well, I have a copy here. [Naur also shows the four aforementioned Pelican books.] They were easy accessible you see, they were cheap too. Definitely, Peter Remnant mentioned Peirce to me, the inventor of pragmatism. My book is dated 1952 you see.

D: In your 1995 book, you have countered Russell's claim that "there are such things as meanings that have one-to-one relationships with words" [59, p.52]. Were you during the late 1950s already delving deep into Russell's writings?

N: No. Definitely not.

[Naur gets some more books from his shelves and shows them.]

Much later, I picked up these books as well on psychology:

- *Criticism and the Growth of Knowledge*, edited by Lakatos and Musgrave, Cambridge University Press.
- Chomsky's *Language and Mind*.
- Quine's *Word & Object*.
- Quine's *From a Logical Point of View*.
- Quine's *Quiddities: an Intermittently Philosophical Dictionary*.
- Ayer's *The Problem of Knowledge*.
- Miller's *Psychology: the Science of Mental Life*.
- Wittgenstein's *Philosophische Untersuchungen*.
- Russell's *The Analysis of Mind*.
- Kuhn's *The Structure of Scientific Revolution*, second edition.

My interest in Quine definitely came from Peter Remnant, but I didn't study it thoroughly until around 1984. I believe Ayer was a student of Russell.

D: I don't think many people in your field read Wittgenstein.

N: I'm sure that Dijkstra admired Wittgenstein.

Russell's *The Analysis of Mind* I got in 1991. In my 1995 book [59] I tried to find out how people wrote about mental life before 1950, that is before computers. I quote Russell at length in my Antiphilosophical Dictionary on perception [60]. Russell is so specific that I easily show how absurd his approach really is.

Kuhn's book I bought in 1983.

D: In the late 1950s you started working at Regnecentralen in Copenhagen. So you had switched from astronomy to computing. That's quite a drastic switch, from the respectful field of astronomy to programming a machine. This looks like an abrupt change in your career.

N: In a way yes, in a way no. For me it was a great opportunity. It was the best thing that happened in my whole career. The new observatory in Sjaelland was in a completely absurd state. It was built to satisfy the ambitions of Bengt Strömgren, the Danish professor who was in charge but who was sitting in the USA for ten years! The people here didn't know what to do about it. It was an extremely frustrating situation. I did some work trying to put the meridian circle in working order, but that was impossible because it was understaffed to an extreme degree. As an astronomer it was extremely frustrating.

At the same time I was a consultant to the **DASK** project. It was in that capacity that I had the opportunity to propose the language of the machine, which was immediately adopted. So I had excellent contacts with them. I had advised them also in techniques to find programming mistakes, along the same lines of what I had done in Cambridge. My experience from Cambridge thus became extremely useful to this group. When I switched to Regnecentralen on the 1st of February 1959, it was very well prepared in advance. I was very happy to get out of astronomy and into an excellent group in Regnecentralen, headed by Niels Ivar Bech. He was the most fantastic leader of this sort of activities that I have ever encountered. That was how I got the opportunity to work on **ALGOL**.

D: You just explained why your expertise from Cambridge was helpful at Regnecentralen. What was the background of your colleagues at Regnecentralen?

N: All the best staff were engineers. Regnecentralen was very much directed towards commercial applications of computing. They had to make a living. Some of my first tasks at Regnecentralen were engineering tasks.

One project was the calculation of radiation fields from antennas. It was related to the American space activity. You have a cylindrical rocket and you want to have an antenna so that you can communicate with it. The idea was to cut a helix around the rocket. The question was how that radiated. There was an expert at the technical university who was able to develop a theory of how the field would be in terms of formulae, infinite series of complex numbers. They wanted to tabulate it, so that was one of my tasks. It was with Bessel functions and all these sorts of things. I didn't understand the theory really, but I could take the formulae and write efficient programs for them.

I also had an application which was with a physicist at the Niels Bohr Institute. He had a very strange integral which he wanted me to evaluate. I did that for him and it was quite successful.

So these were applications that people would pay for. They were all problems in numerical analysis and thus very similar to the kind of things I had done in astronomy. For example, solving the equations of the motion of a planet is a numerical analysis problem. I also taught numerical analysis at the technical university of Copenhagen for several years: integration, matrices, eigenvalue problems, etc.

D: I don't have the impression that you felt you lacked some kind of expertise with regards to programming. It all went pretty well as I understand it. [N: Yes] Pretty soon, after joining Regnecentralen, you met several people on the international scene. You met Bauer, Samelson, Van Wijngaarden, Zonneveld, Dijkstra and others. Many of them were numerical analysts too.

N: They were very much so. Rutishauser in Zurich was very famous in numerical analysis. I'm sure Bauer and Samelson were primarily numerical analysts as well.

D: How would you describe the first meeting you had with these people? You all had a similar technical background, so do you think you were perceived as their equal?

N: No. Not only was I quite a bit younger than most of them, I also clearly felt this central-European professor attitude — professor this, professor that. It is a style that I never much enjoyed and it is very different from the Anglo-Saxon relation. In this regard, I got very well along with Van Wijngaarden from Amsterdam. He was very strong in setting the informal style of discourse for the ALGOL meetings. I wrote a little article on Van Wijngaarden's contributions to ALGOL60 in [45].

D: In 1959 you met Bauer, Samelson, Rutishauser, Van Wijngaarden, and others. Van Wijngaarden made an impression on you in that he set the tone, stressing that everyone was to be treated equally, regardless of whether he was a professor or not. But what about the subject matter itself, did someone make an impression on you technically? Did you feel that you and your colleagues at Regnecentralen were lagging behind technically compared with some of the other European and American players?

N: The ALCOR group (with Bauer, Samelson, Rutishauser) was to me a sort of central-European power play. They said that explicitly. They definitely wanted to be the most influential on the international scene. In the first phase, with our DASK machine, we at Regnecentralen tried to use the ALCOR techniques. That was a useful exercise because it showed ALCOR's limitations. Quite soon, we decided that we could do better on our own.

D: Afterwards you started to collaborate with the Amsterdam group. [N: Yes, much more.] The Amsterdamers were much more in favor of dynamic memory management. [N: Yes] They had recursion, they didn't follow the static approach. Was this technically appealing to you? Did Wilkes's ideas from Cambridge have an influence on your work on compilers?

N: No, not Wilkes from Cambridge. [Pause] The whole thing about dynamic storage allocation — we were forced into that due to the severe storage limitations of our computer. Of course, Dijkstra developed the stack storage of variables.

Then we also developed dynamic storage of the program, which Dijkstra and his colleagues did not consider.

D: Can you elaborate on that? What do you mean with dynamic storage of the program?

N: Well, this was our `GIER` compiler for `ALGOL60`. It could handle the dynamic allocation of programs.

D: Ah, are you referring to what was later called paging?

N: Paging yes. That was invented in Manchester. Jensen picked up the idea from there. We were forced into that because our computer had only 1K working store and the drum. So we developed this paging mechanism, both at run time and at translation time. We made a multi-pass compiler, which was very original. Most people would be proud if they had a one-pass compiler. We said: "Why should you? We have ten passes."

D: So the Amsterdamers didn't go so far?

N: Not on the program, because they had a much bigger store.

The other thing is the checking of the program. We did a much better job at that compared to the Amsterdam group. I think Dijkstra admitted that quite clearly somewhere.

D: Yes. He was impressed by the `GIER` compiler.

We are discussing the early 1960s. You must have corresponded a lot with Van Wijngaarden and Dijkstra.

N: Not a lot. Not a lot. I paid visits to them and they came here at a certain stage. That must have been the spring of 1960; they spent a few days with us. We learned a lot about their techniques: Dijkstra's stack solution of variables and blocks and so on.

D: That's March 1960.

N: Yes, that could be. I also went to Amsterdam at a certain stage and stayed with Dijkstra for a week or so. Well, he came in the summer with his whole family and stayed with my family up in our little summer cottage. So we had quite a lot of private interchange.

D: Did you talk about Wittgenstein then?

N: No, I don't think so.

D: I have here your words, which are about the ALGOL compiler for the DASK:

> [In March 1960, t]he Dutch group impressed us greatly by their very general approach. However, although they were prepared to put their solution of the problem of recursive procedures at our disposal we decided to stick to the more modest approach which we had already developed to some extent. The reasons for this reluctance were practical. [17, 35][57, p.118-119]

For technical reasons, you chose to initially stick to Bauer and Samelson's compiler approach.

N: That's right.

D: I also brought this paper about the ALGOL60 compiler for the DASK. Jensen, Mondrup and you allowed the ALGOL programmer to explicitly express information transfers between the core store and the drum [22].

N: I've forgotten all of this. [Laughter] I don't think I ever ran a single ALGOL program on the DASK. I believe I was in America when the DASK ALGOL was finished and when I came back we immediately started on the GIER project. I had prepared the GIER project in the second half of 1961 in North Carolina where I was research-associate lecturer in the department of mathematics. This was with John Carr III.

D: How was Carr like? He was an older man?

N: No, not that much. He was a little bit... I'm not quite sure I really understood him. On the one hand, he had invited me. But at a certain stage I had the impression he reacted against me — it was hard to say. When I came back to Copenhagen, we at Regnecentralen immediately started working on the GIER project, which ran until August, 1962. While doing that, I also went to a summer school in Chapel Hill in 1962 where I explained our methods for the GIER.

D: Were you inspired by Carr when you were preparing the GIER project?

N: No, not at all. But I did get inspired somewhat by some of the other American projects. For example, using the inverse Polish notation as an intermediate form of instructions during compilation. We used this systematically in what I called pseudo evaluation. We had an article describing this technique [36]. During compilation, you do a sort of evaluation. That is, you form your operands in the stack in the way you would do at execution time, but the operands are not values, they are descriptions of the operands. They allow you to express very simply the instructions you have to produce. It could be used both in type checking (pass 6 in our compiler) and in addressing of variables (pass 7).

D: You were thus much more heavily involved in the GIER compiler, compared to the DASK.

N: Oh absolutely. The DASK was an attempt to use the ALCOR method. Jensen and Mondrup were mainly involved in this. The big problem was storage allocation; they had this 1K and magnetic tapes. It was a three-pass compiler and the second pass was too big for anything. It was very clumsy. The programming was very difficult because they always had to squeeze for space.

D: Maybe your colleagues wanted to stick to the ALCOR agreement, instead of following Dijkstra's dynamic approach, because "the ALCOR train" had already departed and was heading somewhere.

N: The Dijkstra approach was concerned with the stack at run time. While the ALCOR group was much concerned with the translation process and their use of the "cellar" principle. Of course, we took over the details of their "cellar" operations during translation. We had one man, Willy Heise, he had spend some time there and later worked for Siemens. He was in Regnecentralen when I arrived. He had already been to the meeting about ALCOR in November 1958, before I had really joined Regnecentralen. We felt that it was a great help to have their logic for the translation process, and so it was used, but I wasn't concerned with it really.

Before we move on to the mid-1960s, I would like to stress the influence that my numerical analysis methods as an astronomer had on my later work in computing. I started as an astronomer doing computational work. At a certain stage in the 1960s, I had started teaching numerical analysis to engineers at the technical university. My teaching was based on the book *Modern Computing Methods* [30] which is about numerical analysis methods. Since part of my work was making up exercises for my students, I ended up writing the booklet *Twelve Exercises in Algorithmic Analysis* (see Figure 3.1). This booklet contains numerical methods which the mathematicians called numerical analysis and which I called algorithmic analysis. I liked this field very much, I liked to play with it. When we had gotten the ALGOL60 compiler running, I had great fun in using it for experimenting with algorithms published in the Communications of the ACM[1]. I tried them out and this is all reported in the Communications of the ACM. In a sense that was a sort of ultimate continuation of my work in this area. That was why we made a good programming language and compiler, it was a useful tool for our work with problems in this particular field.

---

[1] Association for Computing Machinery

Figure 3.1: Peter Naur's booklet *Twelve Exercises in Algorithmic Analysis*.

4. Mathematical Rigor

D: Around 1964, you also started to study Otto Jespersen's books.

N: That's probably right, given the date I have written down in one of his books.

D: Your interest in Jespersen's linguistic research might have been a reaction to the whole `ALGOL60` project. I have here two papers of yours which are on programming languages:

1. The Place of Programming in a World of Problems, Tools, and People [37].

2. Programming Languages, Natural Languages, and Mathematics [43].

The first paper was published in 1965. The second paper is from 1975 and in it you made an analogy between natural languages and programming languages.

N: That's right. Though during the later 1960s it was mainly a question of formalization. Should we use formal methods in software engineering? That was really the big issue I think.

D: Before discussing some of your papers, I would like to show you the proceedings of the 1964 `IFIP` Working Conference on *Formal Language Description Languages* in Vienna [75]. You were present at that conference.

N: I'm sure that's where Chomsky was mentioned several times. There was this man from Scotland, Fraser Duncan. He quoted me, I'm sure, because he liked that. He was the one who would talk about Chomsky, not necessarily with any kind of respect. "Is your Chomsky really necessary?" [cited from page 298 from the proceedings] That's how Chomsky came into the whole thing. Duncan's presentation from which I just cited was titled 'Our Ultimate Metalanguage' and that's a quotation from me. I'm sure he says that somewhere.

D: Which makes me think of Wittgenstein.

N: No. Metalanguage was a general logician's thing. That is of course how all this language theory came into our universe, which I more or less tried to follow up on. I tried to understand what language really is. I later came to the conclusion that there is no such thing as a language.

D: What about McCarthy?

N: I had very little relation to John McCarthy. He was a very strange man to me. I couldn't communicate with him at all, quite differently from John Backus. I always had a marvelous time with Backus. We more or less saw things the same way. I surely admired him.

D: This paper of yours is from 1965:

- The Place of Programming in a World of Problems, Tools, and People [37].

In it you wrote:

> The programmer should be free to choose this kind of solution [i.e., list processing], but he should not be forced into it.

You were thus already, in 1965, advocating for pluralism: people should be able to choose their preferred method instead of being forced to use one particular technique. We will come across your plea for pluralism again and again as we carry on discussing your research contributions. Do you know whether you already had this urge for pluralism as a child or is it something that caught you in your professional career?

N: I don't know whether it's a basic thing. [Pause] I've experienced, more or less all my life, a certain distrust of formalization, of too much mathematics. Well, it of course goes way back. I can show you a book of pure astronomy by the great astrophysicist called Chandrasekhar (see Figure 4.1).

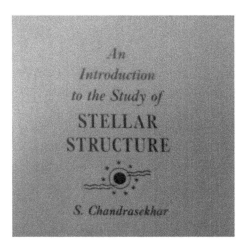

Figure 4.1: Chandrasekhar's book *An Introduction to the Study of Stellar Structure* [5].

That of course was a great book published in 1939. It was given to me by my great professor Bengt Strömgren and I tried to study it very much. Chandrasekhar always stressed rigor, that things should be rigorous. He's most rigorous in a particular chapter which is very long, a hundred pages long. The chapter is on polytopic and isothermal gas spheres from page 84 to 183. That is just playing around with mathematics. You see: mathematics, mathematics, mathematics. [Sigh] It's really useless, but he liked it. He liked to play with mathematics. Chandrasekhar, who was of course a very great scientist, was really a mathematician. That's what he really liked. He's done very outstanding work. Radiative transfer was his later great subject. But his stress on the mathematical rigor always — somehow I didn't really believe it. And it's confirmed because later, at some crucial place in the book, he says that when we are really coming down to astronomy we cannot be rigorous anyway. [Laughter] So I had this mistrust of this belief in mathematical rigor all my life. I studied this book in the early 1940s.

D: People who advocate a lot of rigor are perhaps protecting their research community. They are thinking to themselves: "Look, you can only join us, the elite, if you can be mathematically sophisticated."

N: There is something to that effect, yes, definitely. It's a way of hitting your colleague on his head and saying that he is not really a scientist. Well, of course, we have just the same in programming with formal methods. So I always enjoyed exposing that these rigorous people were mistaken, which I do rigorously. [Laughter]

D: Nevertheless, if I look at your 1966 paper, 'Proof of Algorithms by General Snapshots' [38], you seem to have been inspired by McCarthy's formalization because in it you referred to two of his papers:

- J. McCarthy, 'Problems in the Theory of Computation' [27].
- J. McCarthy, 'A Formal Description of a Subset of ALGOL' [28].

The second paper is McCarthy's work on state vectors which he presented in the aforementioned Vienna conference of 1964. In your paper you mentioned that your general snapshots were related to McCarthy's state vectors [38, p.316]. You described the difference with McCarthy's work by stressing the practicality of your general-snapshot approach:

> However, the present approach, which is directly applicable in proving and constructing practical programs, is believed to be new. Similar concepts have been developed independently by Robert W. Floyd (unpublished paper, communicated privately). [38, p.316]

For those people who have not studied your research papers and who have only read the previous part of our discussion, your usage of the word "proving" in the previous passage may come as a surprise. In fact, studying your research of the 1960s makes me conclude that, during that period, you were very much in accord with McCarthy, Floyd, Hoare, and Dijkstra. For instance, the abstract of your paper is about constructive proofs of correctness. Likewise, in the introduction you wrote:

> It is a deplorable consequence of the *lack of influence of mathematical thinking* on the way in which computer programming is currently being pursued, that the regular use of systematic proof procedures, or even the realization that such proof procedures exist, is unknown to the large majority of programmers. [...]
> However, a reaction is bound to come. *We cannot indefinitely continue to build on sand.* When this is realized there will be an increased interest in the *less glamorous, but more solid, basic principles.* [...] The purpose of the present article is to show in an elementary way that this subject not only exists, but is ripe to be used in practise. [38, p.310, my italics]

To me, this is quite a contrast with your later work in which you basically say that there are no foundations, there is no such thing as computer science, and we must not formalize for the sake of formalization alone. Is it fair for me to make this contrast here?

N: I'm not sure I see it this way. I see these techniques as tools which are applicable in some cases, but which definitely are not basic in any sense. Sometimes it is useful to use general snapshots in this way, sometimes it is not. They are really techniques of documentation, of showing that the algorithm is valid. Perhaps my most convincing demonstration of this is my later work on Turing's universal machine [58], where I used these general snapshots. Until I had invented this way of describing Turing's tape, I could not understand his algorithm. Now I can understand it perfectly. So, it's not a way of proof, it's a way of understanding better. It's a tool for understanding, a documentation aid.

D: When proponents of formalization in computing describe the history of their field, they mention your paper on general snapshots as one of the very first papers that started this quest for mathematical rigor. You were thus one of the first to catch "the formalization train", but you didn't stay on board for very long. You've countered that whole movement.

N: [Laughter] Exactly.

D: I always thought it didn't make sense that this community refers to you as a pioneer for their research. But when I read your paper, I do see a clear connection with the work of McCarthy and others. The same remark holds for your 1969 paper on action clusters [40]. You must have been very much in sync with these people.

N: Well, of course I was. To a certain extent yes. But finally I found somehow that they went too far. It was Dijkstra of course.

D: One final example from your paper on general snapshots, you wrote:

> I wish to claim that *he* [the experienced programmer] *goes through a proof*, and I want this to be brought into the open, ... [38, p.312, my italics]

Do you still stand by these words or are you inclined to say that those words only show how you thought about programming in 1966?

N: My technique is a way of clarifying your understanding. Sometimes it is unnecessary: many programs are so obvious that there is nothing to prove. But sometimes, depending on the problem, there may be a puzzle and then this sort of formal description can be a help.

5. Buying William James's Book

D: In 1967 you bought William James's book, *The Principles of Psychology* [21]. Do you recall when you started reading this book?

N: I'm sure I started to read it then but never all the way through. I'm not sure I've ever read all of it because it is enormously rich. I continue to find interesting aspects of it up till this day. James warns that there are certain parts of it that... He says in the introduction that he regrets there is too much in the book. To understand it properly has taken me years and years.

D: You stayed fascinated by William James because you were not able to entirely grasp it. That's what drives you isn't it?

N: I'm sure yes. For example, finding out how it relates to Ryle was a long and difficult project for me. It took 10 to 20 years to realize that.

D: One of the essential things that William James wrote is that thinking goes on, it is not something that somebody does. Isn't that also part of your 1986 critique of the Turing Test [53]?

N: Yes. But in 1967 I had not yet realized the profundity of this.

D: James also rejected the classical Humean notion of atomic ideas. May I say that he was for holism and against reductionism? You don't use these specific words do you?

N: I don't, but you are of course free to use those words. James used the word "atomism" and I'm sure I picked that idea up sooner than many of his other ideas.

D: Maybe you became attracted to James's work partly due to your strong urge for pluralism. You don't believe in a fixed method of program development that is and will remain superior to all other methods. Likewise, James said that thought is in constant change, it never reaches a state which is identical to an earlier state (cf. [59, p.216]).

N: Every experience is a new thing, we are never the same. We are always changing and we can never understand anything definitely. This whole idea is excellent and very pronounced in James's description of things.

6. Structured Programming

Continued after a short coffee break.

D: Concerning the late 1960s, I see two opposing groups of researchers. The first group, led by Van Wijngaarden, promoted `ALGOL68` as the ultimate programming language. The second group, including Wirth, Hoare, and Dijkstra, wanted to study the methodology of program development and not necessarily defend an "ultimate language".

N: Yes, but Niklaus Wirth's work leading to `Pascal` was clearly an alternative to `ALGOL68`. In the mid-1960s, in one of these `IFIP` working groups, a choice had to be made between Wirth's proposal and Van Wijngaarden's. The choice was made for the latter, that is for `ALGOL68`, which I think was a mistake. I definitely think that `Pascal` was far superior. What happened later, I had more or less let go any way, as I have explained to some extent in [39][57, Sec 2.2].

D: The impression I get from reading your papers on general snapshots and action clusters is that you were contributing to programming methodology. Van Wijngaarden went to the extreme with `ALGOL68`. [N: Yes] Dijkstra, in turn, didn't have a pleasant time either. He got a depression in 1969; he says very clearly in his recollections that he went to hospital [11]. It was not easy for Dijkstra in Eindhoven to create his own group of researchers working on programming. He was surrounded by mathematicians who did not like him or his work.

N: I'm sure he had a difficult time, yes. But I had no contact with him at that stage. It became very direct when I got a copy of one of Dijkstra's writings. I commented back on it by writing him that it didn't ring true to me. I don't think he described what really went on during his program development. He put up a strange myth about how he was working. That's why I wrote this paper about the 8-queens problem [41]. That was a reaction to this, it is a real account of how the program was developed.

D: The paper of Dijkstra you are referring to is his 'Notes on Structured Programming'. I know because you have written about this before. In your words:

> What I find unsatisfactory in the present context is that so many methods and principles of programming are presented without support from systematic studies of their validity or efficacy.
>
> This came strongly to my attention upon receiving E.W. Dijkstra's Notes on Structured Programming in August 1970. Within a few days of receiving this paper I wrote back to Dijkstra: 'This does not ring true to me'. [57, p.395]

And indeed, you wrote about the 8-queens problem in your 1972 paper 'An Experiment on Program Development' [41].

N: That paper was my demonstration of how I had developed that 8-queens program. Of course, maybe other people do otherwise. I don't know.

D: A year before Dijkstra's 'Notes on Structured Programming', your paper on action clusters [40] was published. In that paper you mentioned that:

> This paper may be regarded as a *continuation* of the work in several recent papers (Naur 1966 [38], Floyd 1967 [14], Dijkstra 1968 [7]) concerned with techniques for establishing the correctness of algorithms. [...]
>
> It combines the constructive approach advocated by Dijkstra, and the proof techniques described by Floyd and myself. [40, p.250, my italics]

You were thus still in accord with Dijkstra at that time? Apparently it was Dijkstra's 'Notes on Structured Programming' which made all the difference to you. By 1970 you realized that you did not want to get on the structured programming train.

N: I believe so. That sounds like it, yes. Somehow I couldn't follow them. They made false conclusions from experience I believe. They overstated their case.

D: Programming had to be made mathematically rigorous. Is this not similar to Chandrasekhar?

N: Maybe part of it, yes, yes.

D: Did Dijkstra reply to your letter?

N: I don't think he did.

D: I think you were very close friends in the 1960s, were you not?

N: We were yes. We definitely became split up somehow. That was about 1970. There were other personal reasons which I won't mention.

D: Was William James's book playing any role in 1970?

N: No, I don't think so.

D: Your paper on the 8-queens problem [41] was clearly a reaction to the structured programming movement.

N: Yes, including Wirth. He too went for this approach in his paper on stepwise refinement [78].

D: These papers you wrote, I notice that you are almost always the sole author. Did you discuss your papers with your colleagues in Copenhagen? Did you discuss structured programming with them?

N: Not much.

D: This reminds me of your childhood. It seems your years as a child had already prepared you for later. You were prepared to counter dominant voices in 1970 and take a lonely stance if required.

N: I had been used to that all my life. I had been used to that since my very early childhood. I remember an incident with my parents. I must have been 10 years old, in a stage when I was already interested in astronomy and geography. We were discussing the movement of the earth around the sun. We had a globe in our hand. How does the earth move around the sun? I remember that my father thought that somehow the tilted axes of the earth was the reason for the seasons. In this way I realized that I knew better than my father. [Laughter]

D: That's at a very early age. What about teachers? You must have gotten some negative reactions from them.

N: I was a good pupil. I was always at the head of my class in any subject, more or less.

D: You can be a very good student yet still disagree with what the teacher has to say.

N: Of course, yes. At the age of 15 or so our physics teacher didn't know anything about physics. That was quite obvious. He more or less appealed to me to explain one of his lectures, which was sort of embarrassing and problematic. [Laughter]

I submitted my earliest paper on the calculations of the orbit of a comet [31]. It was published in 1945. It was a calculation of a definitive orbit. Our school had a practice that students could submit research work. I submitted this to my school and it was accepted very much. Then the school would pass it on to a suitable professional, in this case to the professor of astronomy and he made a perfectly satisfactory comment on it. In this way I was known in the school to be somehow way beyond anything. I was invited to give talks, first on Niels Bohr and then on Tycho Brahe. That was in 1945 when Bohr was 60 years old. I also have newspaper articles with pictures of me. [Naur gets the articles from his collection.] You see, in Figure 6.1, "Peter and the stars, the 16-year old Peter has an astronomical paper published by the society of science" — an interview with me when I was still in school. That telescope is sitting in that box over there.

Figure 6.1: The 16-year old Peter Naur.

Figure 6.2: Portrait of the young Peter Naur, painted by his father.

D: Your parents must have been proud too.

N: Oh yes. My father was a painter. Most of the pictures in this room were made by my father. Figure 6.2 is a portrait of me painted by my father.

Figure 6.3 shows me with my father and mother after having gotten my degree at the age of 20, which is very young. I studied for two years instead of the normal five years.

D: How would you describe yourself — as an engineer, a professor, or a scholar? Many people in the field of computing have different connotations for the word "success". What is it that gave you satisfaction?

N: I wanted to understand. That's what gives me satisfaction. What I like best of all is to write and get my clear ideas down in a way that I can stand reading my own work. [Laughter]

Figure 6.3: Peter Naur with his father and mother (13 October 1949).

D: Do you iterate a lot over your writings?

N: Yes, certainly. I always work and re-work and re-read and re-formulate.

7. Empirical Studies

D: You started off in your paper on the 8-queens problem [41] by referring to the work of Dijkstra and Wirth:

- E.W. Dijkstra, 'Notes on Structured Programming' [8].
- N. Wirth, 'Program Development by Stepwise Refinement' [78].

You mentioned that others, besides yourself, had actually questioned the top-down approach of Dijkstra and Wirth.

N: Yes, during the 1968 conference on software engineering there were questions on the top-down approach by Randell, Gill, and Barton [66, p.47-48][67].

D: Not only did you question whether Dijkstra and Wirth's approach works for large software systems, you also criticized their work in two more ways:

- Dijkstra and Wirth did not include direct proofs in their work.
- They did not relate their methodological work with existing work on the psychology of problem solving. For instance, the work of Hyman and Anderson [20]. These authors advocated an "iterative development process".

N: That's right. Hyman and Anderson's article [20] was quite interesting. It was quite influential in my thinking and I used that article quite a lot. They had a handful of problem-solving maxims. I even made slides of it which I used in my teaching. [Naur gets his slides.] Here they are, entitled 'Solving problems'. The maxims are:

- Run over the elements of the problem in rapid succession several times until a pattern emerges which encompasses all these elements simultaneously.

- Suspend judgment, don't jump to conclusions.

This second maxim is excellent. Why should program development be entirely top-down? Why should it be like that? Maybe you should have a combination of top-down and bottom-up.

- Explore the environment, vary the temporal and spatial arrangement of the materials.
- Produce a second solution after the first.
- Critically evaluate your own ideas, constructively evaluate those of others. [Laughter]
- When stuck, change your representational system. If a concrete representation isn't working, try an abstract one and vice versa.
- Take a break when you are stuck. [Laughter]
- Talk about your problem with someone.

The listener can be asleep, it doesn't matter.

I think these maxims are excellent. I used some on my students but that's a long time ago. That's what I'm talking about in my paper on the 8 queens.

D: Did you get reactions from some people, like Denning? He seems to have been countering the whole structured programming agenda [6]. There must have been people who were in agreement with what you were saying, right?

N: Could be. I don't remember any more.

D: You didn't take it personally that there was this mainstream movement which did not match your views?

N: Well, I dropped the IFIP Working Group meetings on programming methodology. I didn't go there because I felt it was dominated by Dijkstra's sort of idiosyncratic approach and I really couldn't stand that. Do you have my review of one of Dijkstra's books?

D: Yes, I have a copy of it here:

- Peter Naur's book review [48] of Edsger W. Dijkstra's *Selected Writings on Computing: A Personal Perspective* [10].

But this critical review is from 1982 while we are still talking about 1970.

N: Yes, but during these ten years I had no contact with all this.

D: In your 8-queens problem you advocated empirical studies. This may be the first time that you did that, though you have done it several times in later publications.

N: Well, recall my booklet *Twelve Exercises in Algorithmic Analysis* (Figure 3.1). That was all about empirical studies and it served as a precursor to my more extensive 1974 book *Concise Survey of Computer Methods* [42]. So I did do a lot of empirical studies at that time, though much of it never got published in articles. I had the ambition to make such empirical studies of a number of algorithms. Well, one of them definitely did get published:

- 'An Empirical Approach to Program Analysis and Construction', Systems Architecture Proceedings of the sixth ACM European regional conference, England, 1981 [46].

In that paper I took the longest algorithm published in the Communications of the ACM, algorithm 414 of Golub and Smith [16], and looked at it carefully. It's a problem of numerical analysis, a question of finding the best polynomial approximation of any given function. I looked into that and found that it had very subtle mistakes, it was ridiculously long and hard to follow. I produced a program which was one third of the original length and where a lot of mistakes had been eliminated. You have an approximation, a function, and a difference between the two which is the error. You want the error to have an equal-height deviation. On the way, you have to analyze bits of the error function and find the local maximum. Golub and Smith did this by taking the numerical value of the function. Therefore, this minimum here [Naur sketches on paper] will turn out to be a maximum. But it's overlooked that such a minimum may actually be on the other side of the zero line. Taking a numerical value of the function is simply a wrong choice. The solution is to apply sign inversion: when you search for a minimum you invert the sign such that you can search for a maximum again. That was one kind of profound error.

Another problem was that their choice of variables was confusing because they did not have an invariant meaning to them. Their variables denoted different things at different times, instead of for instance having what I called clusters.

Another striking thing was the way in which they looked for a maximum of a function. Suppose you have an error function and you want to find a maximum. Then you take these three points and take a parabola through them and ask for the maximum of the parabola. You want to eliminate the smallest [of the four points] and continue with these three because they are closer to the maximum. They had spend something of 30 lines of code to do this because they had named the variables such that they were always alphabetically ordered on the X axis. This forced complicated renaming depending on where the maximum was. This could be completely avoided, resulting in three lines of code!

These are the kinds of things I discussed. It has nothing to do with proving, it has to do with choosing your representations sensibly. The choice of representation is really the key in these kinds of algorithms. And that is an open thing, people never discuss that. How do you choose your variables? Likewise, in our compiler work, choosing our representations was key.

D: You are talking about how to choose a suitable notation as a first step to solving the problem. This creative step, going from the informal problem to the notation, is barely discussed in the literature. Your paper on the 8 queens seems to have been an exception.

N: In my 8-queens discussion I am very explicit about what I start off with. I discuss various ways to represent a chess board and its pieces. The programmer has to realize what these alternatives are and then choose the one that suits his understanding best. This has nothing to do with formal proofs.

D: Your 8-queens paper has, I believe, three take-away messages. They are:

- It's not all top-down; Dijkstra and Wirth were too idealistic.

- Pluralism: "Program development styles have to allow for personality factors."

- Informal before formal: A less formal exploration of the solution possibilities must precede any formal approach (such as action clusters and the associated invariant assertions) [41, p.365].

N: Yes, the third point also reminds me of my account in [59, p.171-188] where I discuss a proof by Gauss and one by Warshall. The proof by Warshall is, again, extremely cumbersome. It's a proof by contradiction so you start with something that is wrong and during the proof you turn your attention to things that are wrong. This is somehow misleading your attention. I presented quite a different algorithm and proof. The crux lies in properly choosing the representations of your problem. To me, that is really what is overlooked by these people. Dijkstra, for example, he starts off with some representation and then I ask "Why this?". He never questions it and we are supposed to take it as obvious that that's the way to do it.

D: What you are saying now seems related to what Dijkstra called "the pleasantness problem" in 1977 and which you discussed in 1989. Dijkstra described the pleasantness problem as scientifically irrelevant [9] and you strongly disagreed with this [55][57, p.474-475]. But we will come back to this later.

In 1974, your book *Concise Survey of Computer Methods* [42] was published. You stated in that book that formal proofs are impractical. The way I view it is that you were making very clear — anno 1974 — that you were not part of the structured programming movement. [N: Yes]

In your 1975 paper 'Programming Languages, Natural Languages, and Mathematics' [43] you made an analogy between

1. mathematics and programming, and also between
2. programming language and natural language.

Regarding mathematics, you mentioned von Neumann's "double face of mathematics".

N: One face for the applications and the other for the pure aspects. Polya comes in my article as well. Polya has been very much concerned with the way mathematicians present their results, they completely cover up all the steps and just present the outcome. That's just the style in mathematical publications, that you don't show how you have arrived at your insight from playing with special cases or something like that. I felt this issue was very relevant for programming as well. Dijkstra, for instance, argued like the mathematician. The descriptions of his program developments are unrealistic to me. I don't think they truly capture how he developed his programs. Again, for example, the choice of representations, where does that happen? He didn't say a thing about that.

D: Assume you were not a programmer but a pure mathematician. If I understand you correctly, you would then be asking your fellow mathematicians to show how they obtained their results, to publish the explanations as well.

N: Yes and I have spoken to Polya about this. I went to California and spend some days there. I believe I was staying with Donald Knuth. He arranged for me to ask Polya about this. Polya said "Yes, yes, it ought to be so, but that's a style of publication, we can't do anything about it."

D: Concerning Wirth's stepwise refined 8-queens problem. There are now two ways I can look at that. One is to say that he did not develop it top-down but that he just presented it like that.

N: I think so.

D: Wirth actually said that himself later, in 1974 to be precise. In his words:

> I should like to stress that we should not be led to infer that the actual program conception proceeds in such a well organized, straight-forward, top-down manner. Later refinement steps may show that earlier ones are inappropriate and must be reconsidered. But this neat, 'nested factorization' of a program serves admirably well to keep the individual building blocks intellectually manageable, to explain the program to an audience and to oneself, and to conduct informal, and even formal, proofs of correctness. [79]

A second way to look at it is that he did in fact work top-down but then only for the small problems, not for the large software problems.

In your 1975 paper you also made an analogy between programming languages and natural languages. To do so, you mentioned Otto Jespersen again.

N: Yes, that's where I really came in with Jespersen. I managed to have his portrait in the ACM. I believe that was the first and last time that a portrait was published in the Communications of the ACM. [Laughter]

D: You used the word "subordination". A formal programming language is subordinate to a natural language.

N: Well, maybe I said that at that time, yes. Later I dropped the whole thing about natural languages because there is no such thing as a natural language. There are habits. You have your habits, I have my habits. There is no language, no English, no French. That is of course really what William James says. If you look at James's work, you will see that he occasionally explains how we understand the word "man" and that it can be understood in such and such a way, but in general he talks very little about language as such. The invention of language is I believe from the logicians in the 1920s or maybe it was from the Swiss linguist Ferdinand de Saussure around 1910. He developed structuralism, claiming that language is a system of signs put together according to rules and so on. Of course, Jespersen made it very clear that that was all wrong: language is a matter of habits. But Jespersen's message is completely forgotten today.

I didn't realize that in 1975. My more explicit concern with language came in later. I had this little popular paper on 'Programming Languages are not Languages' [54] from 1988. There I mention two ways of looking at natural language. One as a system and the other one as a set of habits.

8. So-Called "Artificial Intelligence"

D: Moving to the early 1980s. In our correspondence you mentioned Dreyfus's book *What Computers Can't Do* [12].

Figure 8.1: Dreyfus's first book [12] in Naur's hands.

Figure 8.2: Dreyfus's second book [13].

N: I think this was a very important book on the theme of Artificial Intelligence (AI), a theme I had hated all along. In 1954 I wrote a popular Danish article about the people who said that computers can think and so on [33]. But besides that, I never expressed my misgivings about AI in writing although I did feel extremely uneasy about it. Their general-problem solvers, for instance, they were put forward as the great achievement around 1958. What nonsense! Then Dreyfus's book came out in 1972 (see Figure 8.1). Dreyfus went into each of the AI projects one by one and showed that they never got anywhere.

The AI people always started with a little experiment and
then claimed that it could be generalized in no time resulting
in intelligence. That argument is totally false. They had
what they called a microworld. They could do anything they
wanted in their microworld but it had nothing to do with the
real world. Dreyfus made that extremely clear.

I referred to the second edition of Dreyfus's book in my critical
review [52] of Donald Michie's 1982 book: *Machine Intelligence and Related Topics* [29]. My review was suppressed first.
I had send it in and nothing had happened for a year or two.
I'm sure that some editor had seen his opportunity to put it
in the waste-paper basket. I mentioned this to Jean Sammet,
who was president of the ACM. She was upset of course and
asked for a new copy from me. It finally got published in the
Computing Reviews. That review was the one single case in
which I have received a reaction from someone. That was
from Donald Knuth who sent me a two-line letter saying that
"Very rarely it happened that something in the Computing
Reviews is worth my money, but yours is. Thank you.".

Dreyfus's book was completely silenced, nobody would have
anything to do with it. Michie, for instance, did not refer
to Dreyfus's work at all. Then, 20 years later, Dreyfus's
second book came out, entitled: *What Computers Still Can't
Do* [13]. This book did get the recognition it deserved, it
was published by MIT Press (see Figure 8.2). Of course,
Dreyfus's first book was read too but secretively. It's a long
story.

D: Have you met Dreyfus?

N: Yes, I have met him in Berlin once. Some of his arguments I
cannot quite accept though. He uses Heidegger's philosophy
and I cannot accept Heidegger's argument. This reminds
me of another argument, a valid argument which is not in
my review of Michie's book because I thought of it much
later. It's about chess programs. The AI people like to talk
about chess programs, about the master who plays against a
machine. The point is that the master does not play against a

machine, but against the programmer who wrote the program for the machine. So the master is actually playing against an opponent who has had all the time to prepare his moves, which is entirely against the rules of chess. In chess you have to respect certain time limits[1].

D: Do you have that argument on paper somewhere?

N: I wrote the argument down in 2005:

> Any purpose and choice related to a chess-playing computer program resides with the programmer who designs the program. The purpose of winning is formulated by the programmer as the overall operational structure of the program. The choice of the most promising move must be formulated by the programmer as certain particular instructions in the program the computer is made to execute. Thus it is the task of the programmer to make the choices of the most promising moves for any situation that may arise in the game and to formulate all these choices as instructions, already before the program is put to any use. Thus, since the programmer is not put under any time restraint when making these choices, the human chess player is under a handicap when playing against a chess-playing program. [61, p.19]

D: That passage is from your 2005 book: *An anatomy of human mental life.* Your latest book is: *The neural embodiment of mental life by the synapse-state theory* [63]. Though we will discuss these books more thoroughly later on, it would be nice if you could already say something here. Clearly, there is a relationship between your dislike for AI research, William James's work, and your more recent research.

N: That's right. My latest results are a reaction to all this stuff about knowledge, about knowing, which is very much present in AI. It's very misleading. We don't understand the mind;

---

[1]Editor's note: doesn't the master also have the opportunity to think about the game in advance?

we don't understand the brain. Neurologists have been trying for 50 years with their big machines and scanning, and they have gotten nowhere. I have studied it carefully by looking into a recent encyclopedia on neurology, published in 2003, and reading all the articles about memory. They say that you have a memory; you have a short-term memory, and you have an I-don't-know-what memory, and they talk about these memories, and they never tell anything definite, because they argue, "We will soon find out," and they never find out anything, because there are no memories; there are no boxes. Memory is a delusion.

My latest book (2008) addresses the problem that William James formulated explicitly but which he admittingly was not able to solve. That is, what is life like at the neural level of the nervous system? To put it differently, what Crick and Watson established with DNA at the molecular level, I claim to have done at the neural level of the nervous system.

Part II

9. A Critique of Bertrand Russell's Account of Perception

Five and a half weeks later I visited Peter Naur again in order to continue our discussion.

D: In the 1980s you also read:

- Quine's *From a logical point of view.*
- Quine's *Word and Object.*
- Quine's *Quiddities.*
- Kuhn and Popper's *Criticism and the growth of knowledge*, edited by Lakatos and Musgrave.
- Chomsky's *Language and mind.*
- Kuhn's *The structure of scientific revolutions.*

N: Feeling as an astronomer, as a natural scientist, I tried to understand what science really is. Kuhn had his idea of what science is supposed to be and I studied it. Likewise, I tried to make sense of Popper and his falsification idea. Feyerabend's *Against Method* should be mentioned too. He rejected all these accounts about method. In many ways, I was in sympathy with him. At a certain stage, I wrote my findings down in the last part of my 1995 book *Knowing and the Mystique of Logic and Rules* [59]. There you will find a chapter on the metaphysics of constructed models. Science is a lot concerned with constructed models. That of course is closely related to what you do with computer programming. I pondered much over that in the 1980s.

In my 1995 book I also explain what psychology was like before the era of the computer (i.e. before 1950) by comparing the work of William James with that of Ryle, Russell, Ayer, and a few more.

D: In your 1995 book you wrote that Russell had reasoned circularly. Could you elaborate a bit on Russell?

N: I got Russell's *The Analysis of Mind* [71] in 1991. That book is originally from 1921. It has been reprinted several times so presumably it has been widely read. I noticed in particular that ten years earlier he had produced his excellent paper 'On the Notion of Cause' [73] in which he essentially said that the word "cause" should be eliminated from discussion. Then he continued in this book and talked about cause on almost every page!

There's also the other Russell book, *The History of Western Philosophy* [72], which I've not read until very recently. It is to a large part about ideas of government and political theory, and in these parts I have found it very clear and interesting. What this has to do with whatever is called philosophy is beyond my understanding. Russell also talked about William James and praised him to the skies. He wrote that his psychology was the greatest, but he wouldn't elaborate on it because it is science! Instead, Russell wrote about William James's philosophy of pragmatism, which I can't take seriously. Russell also wrote about the notion of truth, but what is this notion of truth? [Laughter]

I had been reading Gilbert Ryle's work for a number of years before but it was really during the 1990s that I took it up, and I continued to do so for my *Antiphilosophical Dictionary* [60] which was published in English in 2001. There I'm more critical about him.

D: Concerning Russell's circular reasoning, you wrote that:

> Russell ignores that whatever is known as the physical world is known only by way of human experience. Thus in claiming that ordinary human experience, such as the

distinction between perception and imaging, depends on insight into the laws of physics, Russell is arguing in a circle. [59, p.57-58]

N: That looks quite sensible, doesn't it? [Laughter] I have a very clear conception of how Russell discusses perception in his book *The Analysis of Mind* and it's very different from William James. Russell's explanation of perception is in my *Antiphilosophical Dictionary* as a prime example of how this philosophy gets you into deep confusion. Let's look up "Perception" in my dictionary. On page 66 I quote Russell from Lecture V in *The Analysis of Mind* as follows:

> When several people simultaneously see the same table, they all see something different; therefore "the" table, which they are supposed all to see, must be either a hypothesis or a construction. ... It was natural, though to my mind mistaken, to regard the "real" table as the common cause of all the appearances which the table presents (as we say) to different observers. But why should we suppose that there is some one common cause of all these appearances? ... Instead of supposing that there is some unknown cause, the "real" table, behind the different sensations of those who are said to be looking at the table, we may take the whole set of these sensations (together possibly with certain other particulars) as actually *being* the table. ... When different people see what they call the same table, they see things which are not exactly the same, owing to difference of point of view, but which are sufficiently alike to be described in the same words, so long as no great accuracy or minuteness is sought. These closely similar particulars are collected together by their similarity primarily and, more correctly, by the fact that they are related to each other approximately according to the laws of perspective and of reflection and diffraction of light. I suggest, as a first approximation, that these particulars, together with such correlated others as are unperceived, jointly *are* the table; and that

> a similar definition applies to all physical objects. [60,
> p.66, original italics]

This seems impressive at first, but what, exactly, is Russell trying to say here? Concerning the last two sentences in the previous quote: Who or what collects something together? Who or what makes use of the laws quoted and how? It seems that Russell's "different appearances of the table" undergo, through a mental computation process, a detailed analysis, much like the computation an engineer performs when constructing the perspective in a drawing. This computation then has to make use of the laws quoted. For Russell's construction to make sense, his mental computation process must take place without the person's knowing, because people readily saw things around them long before the laws of reflection and diffraction of light were written down! None of us is aware of any computation process when we move around among things.

D: What's wrong with having an insensible mental computation process? If I understand Russell correctly, my eyes register a certain figure, the table, at a certain moment. A bit later, my eyes register another figure of that same table. It is my computation process that compares the two figures and ascertains that they may be understood as two perspectives of one and the same spatial thing, the table.

N: But how can your insensible computation process know which two figures it has to compare? You continually turn your eyes towards numerous things of many sorts. The table is only one of these things. The answer to the question is that the insensible computation process can only go to work if it already knows which two figures belong to the same thing. But if it knows *that* then the computation process need not go to work because the answer is already given. Thus there is no need for a computation process, and no need for knowledge about the laws of reflection and diffraction. Russell's construction is superfluous (beside being impossible) and this conclusion is confirmed by the fact that you or anyone else can readily recognize a table you see on a picture, where you cannot make use of any three dimensional perspective.

D: In your *Antiphilosophical Dictionary* (p. 67) you also claim that Russell is confused in saying that:

> When different people see what they call the same table, they see things which are not exactly the same, owing to difference of point of view, but which are sufficiently alike to be described in the same words [...]

N: How are we supposed to understand "described in the same words"? Even when the word spoken is the same, the sounds brought forth are not, particularly when spoken by different persons. Thus Russell has to assume that people immediately are able to recognize the same word, even in different pronunciations. But then we may surely recognize the same table, even seen from different sides! Besides we are readily able to recognize things even when we do not have designations for them.

I also scrutinized the first part of Russell's passage in my dictionary:

> When several people simultaneously see the same table, they all see something different [...]

When Russell says "they all see something different" he clearly has in mind such matters as the image the person's eye lens forms upon the retina of his eye. This image is undoubtedly different in different persons, even when they see the same table. With his manner of speaking, Russell must understand seeing to consist in the person seeing an image formed on the person's retina. But if this is to be a valid way to understand seeing, it follows immediately that the person has to be equipped with a kind of mental lens that forms an image of the image on the retina, and thus a further mental lens seeing the image of the image formed ... etc. *in infinitum.* This infinite regression, an infinity of mental lenses and images, makes Russell's construction impossible.

Russell's analysis of perception is precisely what they use in Artificial Intelligence, in cognitivism[1]. Perception is viewed as a kind of pattern recognition which is absurd [see Part III]. Russell had this in 1921, long before cognitivism came into computing which was around 1957.

As a further objection it should be noted that if Russell's discussion is to make sense it has to build on the assumption that 'seeing an appearance' is an isolated, primitive experience. His discussion is blind to the experience of the *stream of thought*, which presents to us, not isolated things, but an ever changing panorama of something visible, sounds, touch sensations, smells, taste, visual images, imagined sounds and voices, and more. Normally a person does not see a table, or the appearance of a table. The person will experience a furnished room, with many different things, and in addition a fly buzzing around, a curtain floating in the breeze that is felt coming from the open window, in addition to the mental images, all of them with their fringes of feelings. The experience further includes an immediate awareness of the immediate past and of what is about to take place. So, what has to be accounted for is not how a few appearances of a table are combined, but the fact that the person in this buzzing confusion will distinguish any number of separate parts of the panorama experienced, such as things, buzzing flies, and breezes. Without such an account Russell's theory of perception is void of coherent sense.

D: You just mentioned the stream of thought. Is that what William James wrote about in 1890?

N: That's right. I'm referring to William James's description of mental life in his *The Principles of Psychology* [21]. James's description of perception coheres primarily in virtue of the basic characteristic of mind that James called *the constancy in the mind's meanings*. The mind can always intend, and know when it intends, to think of the Same, something the mind's thought object is acquainted with. The person notices

---

[1]Cognitivism is the idea that the mind works like a computer.

the fly's buzzing, which turns the thought to the same buzzing produced by other flies.

James's description accounts for the perception of definite matters, such as things, by combining the constancy in the mind's meanings with associations. A brief, limited sensation through association turns the person's thought to something already more fully known as a constant meaning, something moreover that the person habitually has encountered in the situation and therefore expects. During the experience of an ordinary scene with things and happenings, the person's state of thought will change incessantly, the attention will jump around. Through this changing attention any matter that is known to be the same as something already known may be distinguished.

According to James's description of perception [21, II p.82] it holds that:

> 'where the sensation is associated with more than one reality, so that either of two discrepant sets of residual properties may arise, the perception is doubtful and vacillating, and the most that can be said of it is that it will be of a PROBABLE thing.'

This may be confirmed at the experience of faulty perception. For example in the dark something faintly and partly seen may be visually perceived to be one thing; then when something more of it becomes visible the perception may abruptly change to something else instead. Both before and after the change the thing is perceived fully, not just as an unidentified appearance.

What is special about *things* in the stream of thought is their relative permanence, a characteristic experienced as a feeling in their fringe in the stream of thought.

James's principle, the constancy in the mind's meanings, accounts for the person's recognition of the sameness of not only things such as tables, but of words, of clouds drifting over the sky, of tones of voice, of persons, etc. By comparison,

Russell's construction is seen to be entirely inadequate by insisting that perception depends on the laws of physics. As a matter of fact, the kinds of changes in the visual appearance, feeling to the touch, and emission of sound, that enter into a person's ordinary perception of the matters in the surroundings of daily life, are far too complicated to make possible even just crude descriptions by present day physics. Physics provides no basis for Russell's philosophical dismissal of the ordinary experience, that people do in fact see such things as tables (cf. [60, p.66-69]).

D: Dreyfus, in an interview [26], has made an interesting observation about researchers in computing, particularly in Artificial Intelligence. If I recall correctly, he said that if these researchers knew anything about philosophy, then it was about the philosophers up and till the younger Wittgenstein. The later work in philosophy, starting with the older Wittgenstein and including Merleau-Ponty is far less known. Do you see it like that? You mentioned that Dijkstra was interested in Wittgenstein, but I suppose this was the younger Wittgenstein?

N: Dijkstra definitely talked about Wittgenstein's *Philosophische Untersuchungen* [i.e. the older Wittgenstein]. I remember him mentioning that, but that does not mean he understood it. As he has explained himself in writing, he couldn't read other people's work if he disagreed with it [10, p.xvi, 148]. So he's not of a source of any real systematic insight really.

D: How do you contrast the younger Wittgenstein with the older Wittgenstein?

N: The early Wittgenstein wrote the *Tractatus*. [Sigh] It's all very doubtful, nothing profound in my opinion. I quoted it in the `ALGOL60` report [1] just as amusement. [Laughter] Later, Wittgenstein did change his mind but not to a sufficient extent. I quoted the older Wittgenstein from his *Philosophische Untersuchungen* where he wrote about the ancient philosopher Augustine [60, p.94]. Wittgenstein misinterpreted Augustine's *Confessions*, claiming that Augustine had said that the meaning of the words is given, 'exists' in the Aristotelian sense, independently of each person's individual, habitual understanding. But that's a distortion of Augustine's account! Augustine explicitly described the meaning of the words as residing in personal habits.

In short, I have only used Wittgenstein's writings to exemplify how the notion of language has become confused, and I have done the same with Chomsky and his generative grammars in [60, p.97].

D: During the past week, I read Jason Baragry's PhD dissertation [2] because he cites a lot of your work. In the beginning of his dissertation he describes your views towards software engineering in 1968. Towards the end, he discusses, among other papers, your 'Programming as theory building' paper [51], which we have yet to discuss. He explains how you were, in 1968, comparing software engineering with civil engineering, automotive design, and Alexander's views on architecture. You were thus, like several others, making analogies between software engineering and other engineering disciplines. Later, you gradually started to pick up and scrutinize the work of philosophers. As a result, your views on software engineering changed. Your theory-building paper is a prime example of this. One of Baragry's take-away messages is that we should look at software engineering in accordance with your later views. You were not the only one, Baragry also elaborated on the work of Bruce Blum. Have you heard of Blum?

N: Yes, he send me his book once, *Beyond Programming: To A New Era of Design* [4]. To be quite honest, I never got down to reading it. What you said about Baragry is very interesting. Maybe Australia[2] will have the next major innovation in software engineering. The USA is hopeless, certainly in psychology.

---

[2]Baragry conducted his PhD research in Australia.

10. A Critical Review of Dijkstra's Book

D: In the early 1980s, you wrote a critical book review [48] of Edsger W. Dijkstra's *Selected Writings on Computing: A Personal Perspective,* Springer-Verlag, 1982. Do you think Dijkstra became aware of this?

N: I suppose so, how could he not? At that stage my relation to Dijkstra had already completely deteriorated over a number of years for certain personal reasons. I had no contact with him. As I wrote in the beginning of my review, I was invited to review Dijkstra's book and I'd rather not have done it. But once I do it, I do it thoroughly. [Laughter]

D: In your review you gave several examples to support your claim that Dijkstra had presented a professional self portrait.

N: The background of all this is the meetings in the IFIP Working Group on Programming Methodology where Dijkstra had been dominating to such an extent that I withdrew from that activity. I couldn't stand it. Some of these IFIP meetings were organized by Randell in Newcastle over a number of years. I took part in some of them. Maybe that was when I picked up the William James book in Newcastle. I still have an excellent relation with Brian Randell.

D: In your book review (p. 270) you also presented a quote of Dijkstra in which he quoted Hoare as follows:

> To quote C.A.R. Hoare from memory 'In no engineering discipline does the successful pursuit of academic ideals pay more material dividends than in software engineering.' I could not agree more.

N: I criticized the words "I could not agree more". Dijkstra had mixed a statement of opinion with a statement of empirical fact.

D: In your book review you wrote that Dijkstra did not want people to use examples in their scientific work but then you mentioned that he had done so himself on several occasions. Dijkstra also wanted to define programming language semantics independent of any computational model, but then you gave examples from his book where he himself talked about "grains of action", "repeated assignment", "number of steps". [N: Yes] Finally, the criticism that Dijkstra got from many people, is that he largely ignored the scientific literature. He did not refer to the work of his contemporaries, as you too mentioned in your book review.

N: Oh I'm sure. He said he was unable to read when in disagreement [10, p.xvi, 148].

D: So it's not that Dijkstra read related work and did not cite it, it's that he was an autodidact. He did not depend much on related work to further his own research agenda?

N: Yes, I imagine.

11. Misconceptions of Program Development

D: In 1982, you had a paper called 'Formalization in Program Development' [47] which was the precursor for the section 'Proof versus formalization' in your 1995 book (cf. [59, Section 3.2]). In your paper you discussed how Gauss intertwined formal and informal notation. Why did you study Gauss's work? Did you already know about his way of working?

N: No. People were always saying "you should be mathematical, you should conduct mathematical proofs". As a reaction to this, I wanted to know how mathematical proofs are really constituted. What could be better than a great theorem by Gauss which I happened to have on my shelf in a collection of mathematical readings? So I decided, there's a mathematical proof of high standing, what does *that* look like? That's why I analyzed it.

D: One of the conclusions in your paper is that formal notation is fine as long as it is embedded in an argument. One should only introduce formal notation if a conceptual gap has to be bridged.

N: Sometimes formalization is useful, and often it's not. For example, in my 1995 book I discussed the example of formally defining a permutation [59, p.187]. Cliff Jones had a big book on formalization [24], and he had defined a permutation by presenting a completely unreadable formal specification:

$is\_permutation(s_1, s_2) \stackrel{\Delta}{=}$
  $\text{len } s_1 = \text{len } s_2 \land$
  $\exists m \in \text{map } \mathbb{N} \text{ to } \mathbb{N} \text{ .}$
    $\text{dom } m = \text{rng } m = \text{dom } s_1 \land \forall i \in \text{dom } s_1 \text{ . } s_1(i) = s_2(m(i))$

Donald Knuth, by contrast, had only needed one sentence in English prose:

> A permutation of n objects is an arrangement of n distinct objects in a row. [25]

D: From your paper I have four take-away messages. The first one, in your words, is that:

> This whole contradistinction between formal and informal techniques is a discussion of a pseudo-problem. [47, p.440]

But don't you need a completely formal description as an end product, so that it can run on a computer? You do view an **ALGOL60** program as a formal object, right? [N: Yes] If I have a description which is partly stated in prose and partly in formal notation, then it can't run on my computer.

N: Maybe the question is whether you are right in saying that what is stated in prose is not formal. Consider Knuth's definition of a permutation, which is in plain English. Is that not a formal definition? In a sense it is. Of course it would be difficult to have a program that will reason from that description but surely it should be possible. It is, after all, put down in terms of black letters on white paper. In that sense it is formal. Every item in his description is supposed to be understood in a precise way. Maybe researchers in computing should face up in accepting this form of description.

D: Your second take-away message is that it is harmful to blindly advocate formal methods.

N: It is simply unproductive to do so. Take Cliff Jones's formal description of **ALGOL60** for example. I took just a half page of his work [19] and scrutinized it in my paper [47, p.442–445]. Understanding that formal specification is extremely difficult, you have to guess what several parts of the specification mean in order to make any progress. It's just not helpful. Dines Bjørner, a close colleague of Jones, has acknowledged this to me. I meet him every now and then in Copenhagen.

Also, advocating a universal formal specification language is troubling, because in practice we use several different forms of notation. Tables, for instance, can be extremely useful in some contexts. So why not choose your form of description carefully? Design is all about choosing your representations and that's precisely what is ignored by the formalists in computing. They never consider why we should formalize our problem in this way rather than in that way.

D: A third take-away message concerns those who advocate formal methods in the name of reliability:

> [There is] a deep inconsistency in the arguments of those who in the interest of reliability advocate the use of so-called formal specifications and at the same time insist on concentrating on what is called the abstract aspects of the problems. [47, p.442]

N: Yes, I gave an example in my paper where the formalists ignore the exact form of output[1]. They would say that it's trivial, it's just output. But that's essential to the reader of the software system under investigation. The formalists assume that reliability is highly dependent on the forms of expressions used in interfacing with those who develop the program, while it is independent of the forms used in interfacing with the eventual users of the programs. Clearly such a view on program development leaves important reliability issues uncovered.

D: A fourth take-away message is that it is not true that program correctness is the most fundamental property of a program, that if a program is incorrect then its other properties (efficiency, fault tolerance) have no meaning [47, p.441].

N: Because if it were true, then it would be incoherent with the large scale software systems that are in use every day and which do have errors in them. My later paper called 'Intuition in Software Development' [50] delves more into these matters. We have to rely on intuition, we have nothing better. It's not

---

[1]The example is from Jones [23, p.308].

a question of eliminating intuition, it's a question of using it in the best way we know. There are no formal principles on how to do that.

D: In program development, you have also subscribed to what I would like to call a holistic approach. You have written that changing a design choice may well affect several parts of the program text [49][57, p.429].

N: Surely, that is quite possible. Why not? Program modification is a profound and difficult matter, which I stress in my 'Programming as Theory Building' paper [51]. Program development is about building up a certain understanding, a theory, it's not about creating a program text.

D: In your theory-building paper you essentially wrote that the program is very much tied to the programmer, that if the programmer leaves the company, then the program is dead. [N: Yes] But how does this work out in practice? Should the new programmers discard the dead program and start from scratch?

N: Generally, yes. It would be better that the new programmers start building their own program. In Denmark we have had one big scandal after the other, scandals about big administrative programs. We have had great difficulty trying to make an accountant system for the university. Enormous amounts of money have been spent trying to maintain that program, just to give one example.

When I joined Regnecentralen, I was asked to design a program to calculate the radiation of a helix around a rocket. The professor there had had a student who had produced a program. They came to Regnecentralen and gave me his program. I looked at it for a few hours and then decided to discard it. No good.

D: You also wrote that:

> [P]rogramming properly should be regarded as an activity by which the programmers form or achieve

> a certain kind of insight, a theory, of the matters at
> hand. [51][57, p.37]

N: Our experience goes like that. Again, our whole experience
with the ALGOL60 compiler for the GIER was very successful.
We sold the design to some American firm. They wanted our
advice on how to adapt it for their specific needs. Initially,
that went quite well but whenever they came to discuss their
extensions, we would be disgusted with the way they had
modified the initial program. Ten, twenty years later that
program, which was still being used by that firm, had been
modified to the extent that it had become a flowering mess.
Although I had documented my methods carefully, it was
hard for them to understand my program. I have written
this in my paper:

> [R]eestablishing the theory of a program merely from
> the documentation, is strictly impossible. [51][57, p.44-
> 45]

D: That means that the programmer loses something when writing
his ideas down in a program text. What does he loose?
Insight?

N: You can say he loses insight. What the programmer has as
understanding is far more general than what can be expressed
in a program text. The programmer has a fringe of relevant
issues that do not come into the text in a visible way, but
which are nevertheless important in the way the programmer
chooses what to write down.

D: In your paper you also wrote:

> [T]he kind of similarity [between program texts] that
> has to be recognized is accessible to the human beings
> who possess the theory of the program, although entirely
> outside the reach of what can be determined by rules,
> since even the criteria on which to judge it cannot be
> formulated. [51][57, p.43]

It's the same with learning to play an instrument or learning a language. You say that can't be done in a rule-based manner either.

N: That's right. The rules can at best serve a descriptive role. The argument that software development is based on a scientific manner is flawed. There is no such thing as a scientific method that is helpful to scientists.

D: But what, then, is the alternative to a scientific method?

N: Common sense! [Laughter] That's how science is conducted. Read James Watson's book *The Double Helix* [77] which is about how he discovered the structure of DNA together with Francis Crick. The first thing he wrote is that the reader will find that his account does not conform to the common philosopher's talk about how science is conducted. I want to quote a bit from his preface:

> As I hope this book will show, science seldom proceeds in the straightforward logical manner imagined by outsiders. Instead, its steps forward (and sometimes backward) are often very human events in which personalities and cultural traditions play major roles. To this end I have attempted to re-create my first impressions of the relevant events and personalities rather than present an assessment which takes into account the many facts I have learned since the structure was found.

Watson rejected all the systematic notions about methods of science. It's very much in accord with my own views. I consider this to be a major contribution to the empirical description of how science really proceeds. I discuss the 18 phases of his discovery in my 1995 book [59, Section 4.1].

12. A Misleading Sketch?

D: I would like to draw a sketch in an attempt to summarize a large part of our discussion. I start with the informal, real-world at the top in Figure 12.1. As you have stressed several times, choosing the right notation is crucial and the first arrow captures this task. I've labelled the arrow as Dijkstra's "pleasantness problem" which I'll come back to later. As you have mentioned, the formalists typically do not pay much attention to this step in program development.

It is the second arrow which the formalists are primarily interested in: the formal apparatus needed to go from a formal specification to a formal program.

As a I draw this sketch, I realize that this may not be the best way to characterize your views after all. The contradistinction between informal and formal is unproductive, as you have stressed several times.

N: Quite. I question whether you will always have to go through this intermediate level of a formal specification. The insistence on such a formal specification, particularly if it has to be in an a priori fixed formal style, is often a burden on

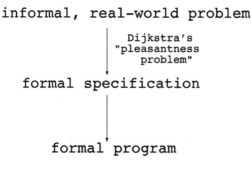

Figure 12.1: A misleading sketch?

the programmer. I discuss this in my 1985 paper 'Intuition in Software Development':

> [R]ules of a method that impose the use of particular, restricted forms of expression on the programmer may in fact contribute to introducing flaws in the software product. [50, p.77]

D: In that paper you also stress the need for intuition at all stages of program development [50, p.75]. So your views are indeed in sharp contrast to Figure 12.1, which is something a formalist would typically draw.

N: I suppose so, yes. The common tendency in the 1980s was to speak of intuition as an inferior human trait. Intuition was viewed to be the cause of major difficulties in program development and it therefore had to be eliminated.

D: In your paper 'Intuition in Software Development', you used Popper's views in defense of your own. You quoted him as follows:

> [E]very discovery contains 'an irrational element', or 'a creative intuition'. [50, p.62][68]

N: Not only Popper, I also quoted Quine, Einstein, and Medawar. So there was plenty of understanding that speaking of intuition as something inferior is absurd. Scientists are supposed to do measurements and look at instruments. But when the meter reads 7.5, how do they know that it is 7.5? That's intuition.

D: Later, in your 1995 book, you distanced yourself from Popper, Quine, and Russell. Did you, in the mid 1980s, already have that thorough understanding of their work as you did in 1995?

N: I suppose not. My critical attitude towards Quine and others came after the 1980s. It often happens that I read something sort of superficially and maybe pick up something and then only much later go into it in great detail. Popper, for example, rejected the whole field of psychology. He refused to have anything to do with it. That was based on his distaste of psychoanalysis, which is very understandable. In the 1920s, Freud was dominating with "the subconscious" and things like that. It must have been disgusting to any scientist, obviously, including Popper. He was so disgusted that any talk about psychology was absurd to him, which I consider to be an overreaction.

13. Syntax and Semantics

D: In your paper about intuition [50], you also wrote about syntax and semantics as follows:

> In much recent discussion of text and language there is a strong tendency to take for granted that in dealing with texts one has to distinguish between things called syntax and semantics, and a corresponding unquestioned belief that the reading of a text must involve separate syntactic and semantic analyses. [50, p.66]

Last month you mentioned to me that the Swiss linguist Ferdinand de Saussure may have been the one who, unfortunately, introduced this in the beginning of the 20th century. [N: Yes] Nevertheless, you also wrote in your paper that this distinction between syntax and semantics is useful in compiler work, in programming languages. Could you elaborate?

N: A "programming language" is an inappropriate term. There is no similarity to the way we normally talk about language. That has been disgusting me all along, right from the beginning in the 1950s when I got into all of this. All these logicians from America, such as Saul Gorn, would immediately come with their formal languages. He had a Baker's Dozen of such languages [18] and that was all based on the idea of syntax and semantics.

D: Did you meet Saul Gorn? Was he a logician?

N: I met him several times. He must have been a kind of logician, I suppose so. He was certainly influential in computing at that time. He wrote his paper on the Baker's Dozen in the Communications of the ACM. I was uneasy about his usage of the term language. Why should `ALGOL60` be called a language? I was always uneasy about that.

D: Yet, you say that in compiler work it is useful to distinguish between syntax and semantics. Why is that?

N: I suppose it is, yes. [Pause] In our early `ALGOL60` compiler we had a number of passes, nine altogether. One may say that the first three were concerned with all that was syntax, because they were described in terms of the syntax notation. Some people used this formal description as a basis of a scanner; to analyze an incoming program. I was never fond of it and viewed it as a rather clumsy approach. At the syntax stage you use letters to identify things, but what they identify is at this stage immaterial. You are only concerned with the delimiters, the symbols in between them, and finding the structure.

Then comes the later processing where you take up which objects are identified by each of these names. That, you may say, is semantics.

D: When you say semantics, do you also mean how the program is supposed to execute? The computational model? For example, the run-time system?

N: It's part of the semantics. The interpretation of the structure in terms of the order of execution, you have to repeat certain things and you have to skip certain things under certain conditions. That's part of semantics, surely.

D: I would associate syntax with `BNF`[1] notation, as presented in the `ALGOL60` report [1].

N: That report indeed distinguishes between syntax and semantics. [Naur takes the `ALGOL60` report from his shelves.] I was sure people would like this distinction. That's why I made it explicit throughout the report. Up here you are only concerned with how symbols are put together (the syntax), down here I explain how they are executed (the semantics).

---

[1] Backus-Naur Form or Backus Normal Form.

Usually I start with the assignment statement, syntax, in terms of BNF notation, then some examples, and then semantics, which explains how things are done.

D: When you just talked about the passes of your ALGOL60 compiler, is the syntax-semantics distinction the same as in the ALGOL60 report?

N: Not really. [Pause] Well, in a sense one may say so.

D: What is your reaction to those people who, in later years, also wanted to formalize the semantics of ALGOL60 and other programming languages? That's what Cliff Jones, for instance, wanted to accomplish with the Vienna Definition Language.

N: I am sure, and Van Wijngaarden very much. Well, that was a demonstration to me, of how you get into terrible trouble. In the case of Van Wijngaarden, the result was ALGOL68, a monstrum of complication. I am sure it is valid, it works because these people were extremely clever, but I don't think it is helpful. It is like Cliff Jones's paper on formalization where he formally specifies a permutation by taking up a lot of space. Putting that next to Donald Knuth's very simple explanation, expressed in ordinary language, shows what I mean.

D: You stressed that syntax and semantics only serve a posteriori. In your words:

> [T]he essential point about such concepts as syntax and semantics is that they are not issues in terms of which a language may first be presented to a person. Rather, they may, at best, serve to bring out aspects of a language to someone who already has the language, intuitively. [50, p.67]

N: Yes, rules are descriptive. It is a form of description of something already known. And describing, of course, is a useful thing. All sciences are about describing.

D: This brings me to your rejection of Turing's Test, which you elaborated on in your 1986 paper [53]. You wrote that if intelligent behavior could be accounted for in terms of rules of behavior, then this would lead to an infinite regress of rules, which is absurd [53, p.179].

N: If intelligent behavior depended on using certain rules, then there would have to be rules about how to apply the rules, etc., ad infinitum. I have also used this kind of argument against Russell which we have already discussed.

14. Dijkstra's "Pleasantness Problem"

D: In the late 1980s you gave a talk at a workshop on Programming Logic. You must have met all these formalists again, including Dijkstra?

N: It was in Göteborg, Sweden. No, Dijkstra was not there. All the attendees were strong advocates of formal methods, and I was invited to give a talk about formalization.

D: You quoted Russell in your paper for that workshop [55].

N: That's right, Russell wrote:

> The fact is that symbolism is useful because it makes things difficult. [74]

D: What does Russell mean with this statement?

N: I believe the idea is that, since formalization is difficult, it forces people to be very careful. You cannot be superficial about these things. You have to really work hard, because they are difficult. [Laughter] Russell was a world authority on the question of formalization. I was trying to understand formalization and the importance of it. Of course, Russell said that this is part of its importance. So, it is an issue which is important to consider. It forces on you to be extremely exact in your thinking. It is against superficiality.

D: So that's not necessarily a bad thing?

N: No, no.

D: In the beginning of your paper, you discussed playing a game like chess. You wrote that, on the one hand, we have the strict rules of how to play the game. But, on the other hand, we should not overlook that the human player has to have the willingness to actually win the game, to play intelligently. So, for the game of chess you made a clear distinction between the formal rule-based part and the informal one, and you stressed the importance of the latter, i.e. the human aspect.

N: That's right. I also quoted Einstein in my paper to convey a similar message:

> [Einstein:] As far as the propositions of mathematics refer to reality, they are not certain; and as far as they are certain, they do not refer to reality. [55][57, p.474]

[Laughter]

Quoting Russell and Einstein was preparatory work, and so was the distinction I made between the formal part of playing chess and the part that requires human intuition. It was preparatory for the part where I scrutinized the research in programming logic as presented at that workshop. To do that, I quoted Dijkstra at length:

> Dijkstra has given a brief statement of his view of programs as constructed models in 'A position paper on software reliability' [9]. In this paper Dijkstra says that 'a computer program is a tool that one can use by virtue of the knowledge of its explicitly stated properties. Those stated properties are known as "its functional specification" or "its specification" for short'. Later he says that 'the question whether or not the program meets the specification can, in principle at least, be settled by mathematical means. The rigorous separation of responsibilities did isolate for the program designer a task that is within the realm of applicability of scientific methods'. [55][57, p.474]

This contradistinction between functional specification and program is what you depicted with the bottom arrow in your sketch in Figure 12.1. Continuing with my quotation of Dijkstra:

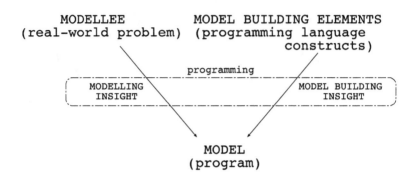

Figure 14.1: My sketch of Naur's views on programming.

> This is later contrasted with '... the unformalized question whether a tool meeting those specifications is in such-and-such unformalized and ill-understood environment a pleasant tool to use. Correctness is a scientific issue, pleasantness is a non-scientific one ...'. [55][57, p.474–475]

So here Dijkstra used the words "pleasantness" and "unscientific" to denote the top arrow in Figure 12.1. I cannot disagree more. For me, program development is all about grasping the relationships between:

- the modellee (the real-world problem),
- the model (the program), and
- the model building elements (the programming language constructs).

D: This reminds me about Chandrasekhar and the discussion we had on mathematical rigor. In fact, you have written it explicitly:

> Dijkstra is insidiously summoning the prestige of science in the support of formality. [55][57, p.475]

I have also drawn the three entities you mentioned — modellee, model, and model building elements — in Figure 14.1. That figure shows how important human insight (intuition) is for you with regards to programming. If I understand you correctly, effectively writing a program text requires human insight in two ways:

1. between the modellee and the model, and

2. between the model building elements and the model (cf. Figure 14.1).

The formal apparatus, of central importance to Dijkstra, Hoare, and Jones, is depicted by the bottom arrow in Figure 12.1. In accordance with your views, this formal apparatus is only obtained from Figure 14.1 if we zoom in on part of the relationship between the model and the model building elements [55, p.473]. Moreover, what Dijkstra called the "pleasantness problem" in Figure 12.1 is crucial according to you and, hence, dispersed throughout Figure 14.1.

N: I would like to stress that the model building elements, which are given, are *tools* for the programmer.

D: The tool, the programmer, and the problem — this reminds me of your 1965 paper:

- 'The Place of Programming in a World of Problems, Tools, and People' [37].

In that paper you discussed the triangular relationship between:

- the modellee (the real-world problem),
- the modeller (the programmer), and
- the model building elements (the tools).

N: Yes, but in that paper I was looking at the whole matter more generally. When you change the tools, say from having no computer to having a computer or from having ALGOL60 to not having a high-level programming language, your view of the problem changes. That too is a matter of human understanding.

D: Dreyfus showed that research groups in Artificial Intelligence abandoned their projects because they were not getting anywhere. It would be interesting to know whether the same was or is happening in Formal Methods.

N: That I couldn't tell you. I haven't had contact with them much. I only got into contact by invitation. I'm sure it was known that I was critical to the activity because I had written a lot about this.

D: How does that work out? You give the keynote address and then immediately leave? [N: Sort of, yes.] I assume most faces weren't smiling when you gave your talk?

N: [Laughter] No, not really. I've been used to this for so long now. Being against Artificial Intelligence was a highly dubious attitude. People were so fond of that great field of computing. So I can imagine they were not too happy hearing me say that it's all nonsense.

D: But they did invite you to give talks?

N: Sometimes, yes. Not often though.

D: You have also written about the subjective nature underlying the formalists' research agenda:

> [I]t is striking, indeed appalling, to how slight extent the results of the formal developments are examined with a view to determining whether the informally stated goals of the activity have in fact been reached.
>
> [...]
>
> It is curious to observe how the authors in this field, who in the formal aspects of their work require painstaking demonstration and proof, in the informal aspects are satisfied with subjective claims that have not the slightest support, neither in argument nor in verifiable evidence. Surely common sense will indicate that such a manner is scientifically unacceptable. [55][57, p.477]

In the previous quote you clearly distinguished between the "formal" and the "informal", presumably because you wanted to express your misgivings in the terminology that was used at that workshop.

N: You are right.

D: You even used the words "sales talk" in your criticism:

> The deplorable situation of programming logic outlined here is part of a much more widespread pattern of attitudes and manners prevailing in academic computing and mathematics, that *tend to accept sales talk in the place of scientifically sound reasoning.* [55][57, p.477, my italics]

This is very ironic given that several formalists considered computer professionals from industry, such as IBM, to be giving sales talk.

N: Right. [Laughter] I even quoted the formalists' sales talk in my paper [55]. They never said whether anything was achieved. It's not clear what the effect of their formalization is. I have documented my claims carefully by quotations.

D: This reminds me of a forthcoming conference in Ireland (summer 2011) which is centered around the theme 'Formal Methods Have Come of Age' [15]. I find this a rather strange title given that that same community organized a conference in 2009 with a small panel on the very last day[1] which heavily debated whether formal methods would ever be used in industry!

N: That [selling of research] has been happening for 30 years.

---

[1]Ironically, that panel discussion (which I attended) is not mentioned in the official program (http://www.win.tue.nl/fm2009/).

15. So-Called "Foundations"

D: At that workshop on Programming Logic you talked about metaphysical superpositions, and you discussed various forms of rationalistic metaphysics in your 1990 paper, entitled

- 'Computing and the So-Called Foundations of the So-Called Sciences' [56].

Could you elaborate a bit on both of these issues? I notice, in particular, that in 1990 you did not only have misgivings about formalization in computing, but about centuries of Western philosophy!

N: That's right. An example of a metaphysical superposition is believing that items of constructed models (e.g. programs) are inherent in their modellees (the real world). In the 19th century, for instance, a common view was that models built upon Newtonian mechanics would account fully for the observable world. Concerning rationalistic metaphysics, I presented four examples in my 1990 paper:

- Aristotelian logic, with the implied claim that human knowing is a matter of truth or falsity of statements.
- Cartesian metaphysics, based on the assumption that valid insight into the world can be obtained by logical inference from primitive axioms, such as Descartes's *cogito ergo sum*.
- The assumption that linguistic activity, that is utterance and understanding of speech, is a matter of application of rules.
- The assumption that intelligence is a matter of application of rules or methods [56][57, p.51].

D: It is here that you explicitly rejected Popper's claim that "science is trying to find theories that cannot be falsified" [56][57, p.51]. I also learned from your 1990 paper that Heidegger had a particular view on how the "sciences" are constituted.

N: Heidegger had this ridiculous view that the level of a science, whatever that is, is determined by the extent to which the science is capable of what is called a foundational crisis. [Laughter] What are the foundations of astronomy or astrophysics? There are none!

D: Heidegger described each science as a building, resting on its foundations. You made an analogy with university buildings.

N: Indeed, the well-endowed universities in the Anglo-Saxon world. The big campus. [Laughter] What one forgets is that these buildings are only a matter of organization. The real research happens across the boundaries. Heidegger's suggestion that scientific fields build on foundations in the sense of a limited set of principles, axioms, or truths, is completely misleading. Even Einstein rejected this idea. I explain all this in my paper.

D: This also clarifies why you dislike the words "computer science". [N: Yes] In your paper you also elaborated on rational metaphysics in the field of programming and, not surprisingly, referred to Dijkstra's research agenda and his "pleasantness problem" described in Dijkstra, 1977 [9]. In your words:

> [M]uch of the work published as contributions to computer science is deficient. Most prominently, inventions, in the form of programs or systems of notation, are presented without adequate support from [...] investigation. Commonly the inventions are presented with the support of an analysis of their purely formal properties, while their informal properties, particularly how they support the persons involved, are treated scantily or not at all. Such a treatment would conform to a *rationalistic metaphysics*, the assumption that the world can be understood fully in terms of the truth or falsity of statements.

[...]

A closely related circumstance is the common adoption
of a rationalistic metaphysics, which declares that only
formal questions are scientifically relevant [e.g. Dijkstra,
1977 [9]]. Whatever the reason, most computer-based
models and tools are promoted, not by scientifically
supported evaluations, but by unfounded postulates
and claims [...]. [56][57, p.56-57, my italics]

N: A publication on these matters is called 'Computing As Science'
which you can find as Appendix 2 in my 2005 book [61]. Every
science is a matter of description. Such things as mathematics
and computing are of course auxiliary to physics and so on.
You use these as forms of description in the various sciences.
That's the place of computing.

D: Just to be clear, when you say "science" here, you most
definitely do not mean a pillar with a logical basis à la
Heidegger.

N: Right, science is just a field of coherent descriptions. In the last
part of my 1995 book [59, Section 4.6] I discuss a very wide
range of fields and show that choosing the right description
has always been the key to scientific progress. These fields
are depicted in Table 15.1. I used the words 'organized
knowledge' to explain that table in my book, but today I
would much rather write 'communal activity fields' instead
of 'organized knowledge'.

Coherent descriptions as being the core of science is my rejection
of the unconscious and a counter to Popper and Kuhn. As
I have mentioned before, Popper with his logic completely
rejected any talk about psychology. The first thing Popper
wrote in his book [68] was:

A scientist, whether theorist or experimenter, puts
forward statements, or systems of statements, and tests
them step by step. [59, p.293]

But it's not like this at all. Watson and Crick's discovery of
DNA's structure, for example, was not a matter of true

statements. None of the experimental facts obtained by Watson and Crick and their contemporaries were solidly correct. Each of them were taken as merely plausible clues that might be in need of further confirmation or revision. Watson adopted statements that described the *overall* features of the structure, his issues of concern had no statements that were tested in Popper's so-called step-by-step fashion. Watson and Crick's result, the molecular structure of DNA, cannot be claimed to present a correct statement either. A model of the structure of a molecule is just one kind of description of the substance under investigation, well known to ignore certain aspects of the actual substance (cf. [59, Section 4.1.5]).

D: Why did Popper insist that scientific discovery must be understood primarily as a matter of true statements?

N: Because he loved logic. That's what it is, philosophical prejudice. My investigations show that science has nothing to do with logic or truth. It is merely a matter of description. Descriptions are not true, never, they are more or less adequate. That's the best they can offer. They are useful. Truths are not useful. [Laughter] This goes all the way back to William James.

Popper also had the notion that scientific discovery is a matter of theories which can be falsified by the activity of the scientist. But, again, this does not apply in Watson and Crick's case, just to give one example. Their DNA structure cannot be described as a theory and establishing that structure can hardly be said to contribute to theories one way or another. The relation is that Watson and Crick's model of the molecular structure of DNA, to make sense, presupposes a whole range of theories of physics, chemistry, and biology. What the model contributes is additional coherence of these theories. However, coherence is not a matter of truth or falsity.

Concerning Kuhn, his way of describing matters depends entirely on the notion of scientific theories or paradigms as things that have to be accepted or rejected as indivisible units. But what are these paradigms? There are no such things, neither in Watson and Crick's case [59, p.249], nor in Kuhn's own account on the 18th-century hypothetical principle of fire [59, p.298].

According to William James's views on human thinking, it is the occurrence to the thinking person of striking associations of similar objects that makes scientific discoveries possible.

| Area of concern, | Activity, by kind | | |
how accessed or formed	Descriptions	Forecast	Typical action
Public, repeatable pheno- mena of surroundings	Physics, chemistry		Construction, building
Language, formed by collective invention	Linguistics, dictionary, grammar		Talking, writing, language teaching
The universe, what is observed in the sky	Astronomy	Visibility of Sun, Moon	Navigation at sea, in space
The air we find around us	Meteorology	Weather	Aviation
The publicly observable ground under our feet	Geology, geophysics	Earthquake warning	Mineral pro- specting
Invented formal structures	Mathematical theorems		Mathematics application
Automatically processable formal structures	Computing		Programming
Publicly observable life other than human beings	Botany, zoology	Nature pre- servation	Agriculture, livestock culture
The publicly observable communities of humans	Sociology, history	Population growth	Public policy, law enforcement
Human consciousness, as accessible to introspection	Psychology, novels, biography	Conduct of personal life	
Public works of art and music	Aesthetics of art and music		Artistic creation and performance
Buildings for human shelter and use	Architecture		Buildings, design and construction
Publicly accessible consti- tution of living organisms	Biology	Epidemic warning	Health care
Religious beliefs as ac- cessible to introspection	Theology		Worship

Table 15.1: Areas of activity involving communal activity fields [59, p.319].

16. Understanding Turing's Universal Machine

D: In the early 1990s you tested whether a description found useful to one programmer was equally useful to another programmer, by having your students study Turing's 1936 paper [76]. You wrote your findings down in:

- Understanding Turing's Universal Machine — Personal Style in Program Description [58].

I am curious why you chose Turing's paper for this project.

N: Turing presented a program in his paper which is totally different from what we have today. Of course, he didn't have anything better, he invented it all on the spot by his genius. Just understanding that is a challenge to any present-day person, a challenge which was a good way of having people think about program understanding. I've known the existence of Turing's 1936 paper for decades. I had glanced at it several times throughout my career and saw this strange symbolism with ancient German notation, altogether completely different from what we have nowadays. At a certain stage, I decided that I had to read and understand it, and I could only do so by adding to it a formal description. I had to invent a supplementary description of his program, which is not in his work, so that I could formally describe the states of his machine in certain terms. This description is also explained in my 1995 book [59, p.198]. It's a snapshot representation of Turing's machine, inspired by my paper on snapshots from the 1960s [38]. As a result, I could make formal demonstrations of the correctness of his program. Then I challenged my students by asking them to develop a description that they would find helpful in understanding Turing's program. Furthermore, while doing that, they were asked to indicate the mistakes that are present in Turing's program. I found that this was a useful course activity with the students. It gave the challenge to test out whether formal descriptions appealed.

The course activity had two phases. In the first phase, every student had to study Turing's program and formulate an additional description that would help other people understand Turing's program. Every student would then submit a report, and then I would mix into that my own report which they were not aware of. All reports were anonymous. In the second phase, everyone had to look at all the other reports and note down whether they found them to be clear and helpful. In this way, I forced them to look at my very formal description, which was somewhat unique compared to the other reports. I was curious how people would react to it. I found that the reaction to my description was very much person dependent. Some students considered it simply hopeless. Others thought it was a great aid. That shows something about the personal aspects of understanding.

As you can read from the introduction of my paper, my purpose to do this project was two-fold:

> The primary purpose of the present study is to present some empirical evidence related to the programmers' understanding and their use of descriptions in computer programming. Key issues are the importance of individual style differences and of formalized descriptions in programming. A secondary purpose is to demonstrate a technique for empirical investigation of issues of programming. [59, p.189]

Empirical evidence was what I wanted. The conclusion is that some people like formal descriptions and others don't. It's a very personal matter. There's no middle way so to speak.

D: You're saying that each individual has his or her own preferred style of program development. But is it possible that there are, say, at most ten different styles?

N: No, my style, for instance, was developed solely for Turing's program and served no other purpose. For another program, I would very likely develop another style.

D: It is Turing's original 1936 paper that you gave to your students. [N: That's right.] That paper also interested you a lot, you wanted to finally get down to understanding it.

N: Yes, and it should also interest the students because it is a fundamental paper of the whole field and it is unknown. Nobody knows about Turing's paper. I've talked about this in working conferences in the United States. This is the most famous paper in computing, and I asked how many people in the audience had ever read it. Nobody. [Laughter] That's what it is like.

D: I think you may be one of the few who has actually read his paper.

N: Probably. And of those who were aware of his 1936 paper, very few understood the difference between a Turing Machine and the Universal Machine. Many people have mixed up the two, thinking that a Universal Machine must be a Turing Machine. Any computer you see in this room is controlled by a program and thus is a Universal Machine. In this way you can simulate any other machine's program by programming.

D: Was it difficult to organize such a project at the university?

N: No difficulty at all.

D: In your paper you wrote:

> On this background, one relevant question is whether there is a clear correlation between the formal properties of the description forms used by a programmer and the understanding achieved by the programmer. [58, p.351]

N: The understanding achieved was partly measured in terms of the number of errors found by the students. Some of the students, themselves, introduced and used their own formal notation. Others used examples, which can be quite effective too. That's what Polya would say: start with concrete examples and then get the knack of it. Some did step-by-step execution of the program which is reasonable if you are completely unfamiliar with Turing's program. They would then get stuck rather quickly, because there is an error in Turing's paper which entails that you will get stuck rather quickly if you follow a step-by-step approach. One of the students did get stuck and could not continue reading Turing's paper. [Laughter]

D: These errors that Turing made, can't they all be easily resolved?

N: Some of them, not all of them. There were some subtle errors. I listed all errors in my paper and I discussed the corrections [58, p.353]. The list also shows who corrected which errors, again showing the individuality of such understanding.

Part III

17. Neural Embodiment of Mental Life by the Synapse-State Theory

D: Let's discuss your 2008 book, *The neural embodiment of mental life by the synapse-state theory*[1] [63].

N: The first chapter is an introduction in which I mostly present what you will find in the Encyclopedia of the Neurological Sciences (2003). I then compare that with William James's work [21] which was published in 1890. I explain that what is presented in the encyclopedia is merely a lot of confusion and unclarity, centered around the idea of memory as a container. In the encyclopedia you will find six or seven articles about memory, short-term memory, long-term memory, and I-don't-know-what memory. If you look into these articles you will find that all they do is express bright hopes, they never present any results. I also discuss the many other articles about aspects of mental life, such as attention and language. But there is no language, only habits. Talking about language is just confusion. There are articles on instinct, the motor activity, intelligence, feelings, and plasticity. The articles on feelings are rudimentary, only covering the feeling of pain. All the extremely important feelings which are central in human existence are unknown. Concerning plasticity, the authors don't understand what it is, they don't use the word plasticity in its proper meaning. So that's the first chapter, a sort of rather thorough critique of what you find in modern

---

[1]See also Naur's 2005 Turing Award lecture [62] and his recent invited talk at the conference 'Click-on-knowledge 2011: Web-based knowledge and Contemporary Scholarship' [65].

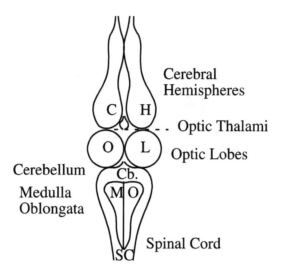

Figure 17.1: The frog's nerve centres [63, p.31].

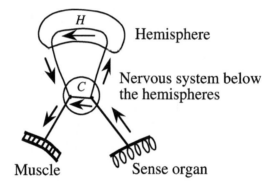

Figure 17.2: Circuits of the nervous system [63, p.33].

literature on the subject of the neural system and how it works.

D: For that first chapter you delved into the vast literature and explained why it's basically not adequate. [N: Yes] Let's carry on to the second chapter.

N: In the second chapter I present what is mental life and the synapse-state theory. That theory is centrally based on William James's *The Principles of Psychology* from 1890, which I consider an absolute masterpiece. The first figure here (Figure 17.1) shows something about the nervous system of a frog. Experiments on frogs allow us to see that there are two sections of the neural system: the lower centres and the cerebral hemispheres. In the experiments with the frogs, researchers found out that reflex movements, which we all have, only go through the lower centres. Voluntary movements, on the other hand, go through the cerebral hemispheres. As James wrote very clearly, "processes become organized in the hemispheres which correspond to reminiscences in the mind" [63, p.33]. Something coming in through our senses goes through, somehow, the hemispheres and gives rise to our voluntary movements. Figure 17.2 reveals James's structure: reflex movements happen in the lower centres and voluntary activity takes place in the upper part. What happens up there? What are the hemispheres like? How can the hemispheres hold reminiscences, vestiges of past experiences which influence our actions? That's what James wanted to find out. He discussed this carefully and decided that he could not answer these questions. He had some sketches which he admitted were not adequate. He wrote very clearly that these questions were for the future.

D: Figure 17.2 shows two pathways through the nervous system. Was this figure James's contribution or was it already known?

N: I suppose it was already known. I don't know who exactly formulated it like this. Maybe it was Meynert, the Austrian physiologist, who also sketched some other theories which James quoted. There was a whole generation of excellent neurologists at that time who found out an enormous lot of things from about 1850 and onwards. It wasn't all William James. Even back in 1830 Marshall Hall, an English physiologist, discovered how reflexes go through the back spine. That was rejected by the Royal Society of London. They would not publish "such nonsense", as is typical of great discoveries.

D: Chapter 2 in your book starts with having a look at what James had to say about the upper part in Figure 17.2.

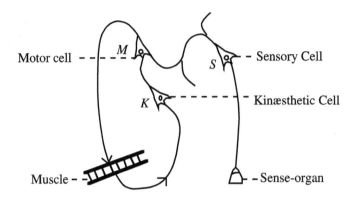

Figure 17.3: Muscular control by the Meynert scheme [63, p.40].

N: About mental life in general, how the stimuli somehow are handled in the system. James had various principles. One of them is the *summation of stimuli*: in order to release an action you often have to have several influences coming in. Another principle is the *law of diffusion*: every influence on the nervous system somehow propagates through the whole body. These are some of the general features which James discussed.

Then of course the question is: how are habits developed? Habits are fundamental. As James wrote, every organism is a bundle of habits. That is completely unknown in modern psychology! How do you educate habits? Well, how do you educate the nervous system? Figure 17.3 is a sketch, a Meynert scheme. James tried to understand it properly and concluded that it was not really adequate. Then come several pages about experience, the matter of being a live person and experiencing something, experiencing the stream of thought or the stream of consciousness. James described this in great detail and that is one of the most interesting, important, and difficult subjects there are. Everyone of us has an enormous amount of experience at every moment, what we see and somehow feel. How to make sense of what James called the stream of thought? James found a number of features and properties of the stream of thought, which is central in order to understand what is going on in the mind. That is one of his greatest contributions.

D: Was it recognized as a contribution in his time?

N: Absolutely. James's work was extremely famous in his own time, and for several years after everyone agreed his work was a classic. But from 1913 it was pushed aside when behaviorism started. The behaviorists claimed that you cannot verify what people say about the stream of thought, it is unobservable, you can only observe it yourself, therefore it is not scientific! So behaviorists didn't talk about it at all. Because of this, psychology has been lost for a hundred years now.

D: Was William James still around in 1913?

N: No, he died in 1910. It was a Mr. Watson who made this idiotic claim, the later president of the American psychological organization. He became completely dominating so that you could not discuss anything dealing with the experience in conscious life. You could only do experiments with people treated as objects where you push them and then see what happens, and never ask what they experienced. That has been dominating now for a hundred years.

In my book I continue discussing James's views on sensation and perception. These are subtle matters, we sense things but we also perceive things. The distinction is important and James clarified it in a masterly way. Sensation is to see that there is red, there is blue. Perception comes into play when we see things with which we are familiar, what we are acquainted with. James didn't talk about knowledge, he talked about *knowing about* and *knowing by acquaintance.* These are the two aspects of the relation of knowing. It is possible to be acquainted with something yet know nothing about it.

Attention is concentration in our stream of thought on a particular thing, for example something we are acquainted with. How that happens is explained next in my book. James also discussed specious present, the feeling of now. We give attention to the present, but a moment later we also, in a sort of weakening form, give attention to what we were attending to a minute or two ago. That lingers on in our stream of thought. James called this the specious presence to emphasize that presence is not a sharp moment, it is a certain duration of about a few minutes, allowing us to sort of combine in our thinking the things which are there now and which were there a few minutes ago.

Retention and recall is discussed on pages 49–50 in my book. There is no memory, no box. It's just a matter of excitation of particular things that we are acquainted with. Recall is calling forth what we have been acquainted with earlier and for the moment have not been thinking about.

D: So, it's not that somewhere in my brain I have stored the equation $5 \times 4 = 20$?

N: When you formulate the two numbers with the multiplication, they are combined and then the answer comes. It was there all the time but it was not at your attention. There is a lot of stuff which is not present in our attention, we can only attend to a few things at any moment. People often talk about the subconscious or the unconscious; Freud's work may be the reason for that. And, indeed, there are lots of things which we might think about yet we don't think about now. But it's not just one continuum, we have lots and lots of different, maybe hundreds or thousands, of different unconsciousnesses. Each unconscious corresponds to a particular moment of our previous experience. We attended such a place and we met such a person, and that is then hidden away. These things are all concentrated in situations. The present situation is one which is now our active present, but there are many others from the past and they can be called forth by hypnosis.

Concerning hypnosis, there is nothing mysterious about it. Hypnosis is just reactivating situations which have not been activated for maybe years. Yet, you can pull them forth. A good hypnotist can, by subtle techniques of talking to

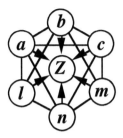

Figure 17.4: Recalling a thing forgotten [63, p.52].

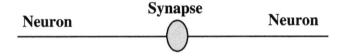

Figure 17.5: Sherrington's synapse connection [63, p.54].

the patient, make them forget the present for the moment. That's what hypnosis is, which is covered in the last chapter of my book.

Figure 17.4 shows that if you try to remember something, you have to think of clues. For instance, if you want to recall the name of a particular person, you can ask yourself where you have met that person, what you had discussed with him, and so on. By thinking about such clues which are relevant, we can perhaps recall the particular person's name. It's not because it was not there, it's merely that you didn't have it activated at the moment.

D: The next important topic in Chapter 2 is the work of Sherrington.

N: Indeed. Sherrington was a great English physiologist, who studied the behavior of dogs. He discovered a feature of the neural system which he called synapses. They are connections between neurons. Two neurons can transmit excitations to each other via an in-between synapse, as shown in Figure 17.5. The synapse is a sort of break on the traffic of the excitations. The crux is that a synapse is plastic and that's exactly what we need to acquire habits.

D: When you say plastic, it certainly means it's not digital, right? That's one of the implications.

N: More than that. It is like the sculptor who puts his thumb in the clay in order to change the shape of the clay. That change of shape stays there, it's what is not elastic, it's plastic. It changes by the influence you put on it. Synapses, when they get subjected from neurons on both sides by means of excitations, change and get more conductive in a plastic way. Maybe two neurons have been excited many times, then, gradually, they become connected by means of a synapse, as in Figure 17.5. When you activate one of the neurons in the figure, you more or less automatically activate the other one as well. That is how items, things with which we are acquainted with, get combined in our thinking.

D: Is it all reversible? Can I acquire a certain habit and then completely loose it again?

N: In time, if left in peace, the synapses will become less conductive. This can take years, depending on the kind of synapse. The synapses related to the muscular movement have a much shorter time scale. If you train a movement, like the particular movement of a tennis player or a musician, then you can become extremely expert in doing it. But no practice for a week can rapidly deteriorate your performance.

The synapses of the motor layer are depicted in the lower part of Figure 17.6, beneath the item layer which is in the middle and the sense layer which is at the top. The figure shows the total structure of the nervous system, which consists of three elements: the synapses, the neurons, and the nodes. The neurons are depicted by lines and the nodes are depicted by rectangles. As you can see, large numbers of neurons come together in the nodes.

The central part of the figure depicts the item layer. Each node in the item layer is connected to any other node through one synapse. For example, Node A is connected to Node B through synapse ITEM-AB. Now, if there are about, say, a

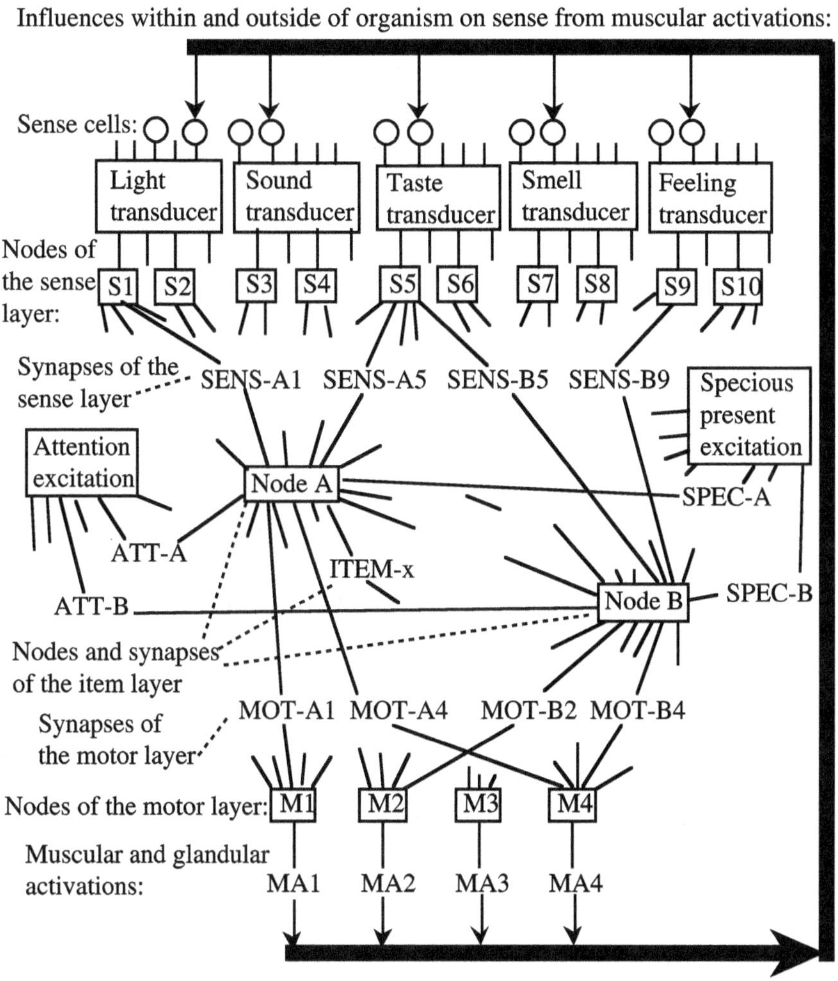

Influences within and outside of organism on sense from muscular activations:

Figure 17.6: The structure of the nervous system [63, p.55].

hundred thousand such nodes, then there would be something like five billion synapses. Each of these synapses will be in a state of conduction, which changes in a plastic way depending on the excitations of the corresponding nodes. These nodes get excited from all sorts of things and the excitations combine in the node by summation. At any moment, one node will be influenced by a certain number of other nodes through the neurons and synapses. How many depends on the state of conductivity of the synapses.

D: The synapses are the only plastic elements?

N: That's right. The synapses are the things that change in the brain by time. When you learn things, only the plastic states of the synapses change.

D: Is the relationship between the plasticity of a synapse and the acquisition of habits part of your research contribution?

N: Certainly, and Figure 17.6 is the central contribution of my synapse-state theory. It illustrates how the structure of the nervous system in the brain is constituted. In the center of the figure we have the item layer which is where attention happens. Attention means that one particular node of the item layer is strongly excited. First a node, say Node A in Figure 17.6, gets excited from various other sides. If the total excitation of Node A exceeds a certain level, then a special synapse (ATT-A) connected to Node A gets an excitation from a special source of excitations. This source is labeled "Attention excitation" in the center left of the figure. It releases into Node A a very strong additional excitation which then makes Node A the center where the attention sits. But, this changes from second to second — the excitation lasts only about a second or two. Meanwhile, other things go on as well. I will use Figure 17.7 to explain that.

Figure 17.7 is a typical picture of a momentary excitation pattern. You have one node, C, where the attention sits. It gets a lot of excitation through synapse ATT-C and maybe from other sources as well. But there are other nodes, B, A, I, J, K, ..., some of which have been strongly excited a few seconds ago. They have excitations also coming from the specious present excitation source, depicted in the center right of the figure. The result is that there is a sort of queue of falling off of nodes where the attention has just been which constitutes the specious present, what is sort of half way present when the attention is at C. In this way the whole pattern of excitations in the complete structure is in

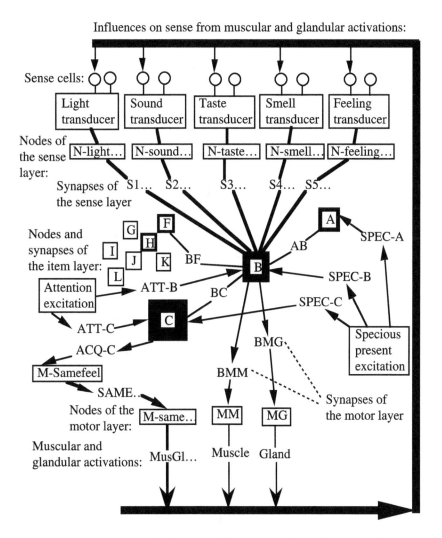

Figure 17.7: Embodiment of thought object [63, p.59].

continuous change. There are lots of other nodes, such as I, J, K, L, that have much much weaker excitations; there will be at any time a hundred or thousands such nodes which constitute what James called the fringe. James has very much discussed the weak influences in the stream of thought, the fringe of weakly perceived parts of the stream of thought.

Meanwhile, we shouldn't forget about the senses, depicted at the top. The sense cells will, through special transducers (for light, sound, taste, smell, and feeling) send excitations into nodes of the sense layer. Each of those nodes is, again, connected to all nodes of the item layer through sense synapses. So that when we see something, there will be an influence on the sense cells, going through the light transducer and the nodes of the sense layer (N-light...), and then, depending on conductivities of the synapses (S1...) which go to the nodes of the item layer, there may be a special combination of excitations corresponding to a particular thing like the face of a person. When I see a particular face, that would lead to quite particular excitations of this set of nodes (N-light...). And then, if I recognize the face, there will be one node, B, which corresponds to my thinking of that person. That node B is connected to the set N-light... of nodes by conductive synapses of the sense layer (S1...). That is how perception happens; the conductive synapses of S1... pick out from the enormous number of nodes in the item layer just that particular node B.

Sensation only leads to excitations in the nodes of the sense layer. That is where our sense experience is. When the nodes of N-light... are excited, we see light. When the nodes of N-sound... are excited, we hear sound. We can have all these sense expressions without perception. The latter will only take place if the synapses pick out a node in the item layer.

D: Let's assume I'm in a classroom and the teacher writes 5×4 on the blackboard. I assume that, in my case, perception will be involved. [N: Surely.] How would that work out?

N: There will be perception of 5 and perception of 4. There will be two nodes in the item layer, one for 5 and one for 4. Likewise for the multiplication sign. It becomes very complicated to depict graphically. A lot of nodes will come into play, including the intention that you want to combine 5 and 4 and make use of certain combinations that if you have these two they will, through their conductive synapses, also influence the figure 20. Because that's the habit when you see 5 and 4 and the invitation to do a multiplication. These two figures and the multiplication sign, each as a node in the item layer, will have conductive synapses going into 20. So there will be a summation of three strong impulses into the figure 20. Then you can speak out the result 20.

D: How do we speak?

N: That's a matter which concerns the motor layer, depicted at the bottom in Figure 17.7. There are muscles and glands, each of which is connected to one node of the motor layer. The nodes in the motor layer, in turn, are connected through conductive synapses to the nodes of the item layer. In this way you can, from excitations up here, excite these nodes and get excitations of muscles. But, again, it is a matter of combining things before it really happens. To speak, for example, I need to use my muscles and have the intent to speak. Both are required and then, by the summation principle, I will speak. The summation principle is fundamental in the whole activity of the nervous system.

Another thing which I want to point out is this thick black arrow which represents the connection in our tissue (our muscles, arms, fingers, ...). The black arrow indicates that our muscular movements influence our sense cells which, in turn, influence the nodes in our item layer, as explained previously. In this way, what we do with our muscles immediately gets registered in the senses and, by means of combinations, allows us to continue with our movements.

D: This is also why mind and body are not detached.

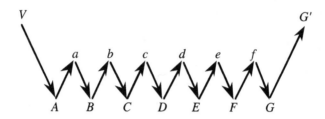

Figure 17.8: Habitual chain of muscular contractions and sensations [63, p.36].

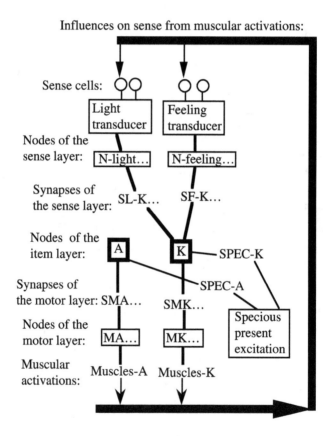

Figure 17.9: One step in muscular control from A to K [63, p.67].

N: Exactly, they are completely integrated. You cannot divide them at all. That is essential in most of the actions we do. In my book I discuss James's account of habitual actions by means of his Figure 17.8. Suppose I want to take a drink from the cup on the table. To do so, I move my arm, grab the cup, move my hand to my mouth, etc. That's a series of submotions which follow each other habitually. Such habits are simply matters of the synapses which have been educated in the nervous system. In terms of the figure, my first action is A. And, as a result of this happening in my muscle, the result is a sense a in my sense cells which releases the next action B, and so on. Because my movements are well trained as a habit, the whole thing rattles off and I don't have to pay attention to it.

It is typical in speaking. Figure 17.9 shows two actions A and K. You start with the excitation of A, follow the arrows in the figure, and you end up with the excitation of K in the item layer which, in turn, results in the activations of Muscles-K. In speech, everything is a series of syllables and each syllable will be one node in the item layer, such as A and K, which releases one set of contractions in your muscles.

Figure 17.10 illustrates perception and what James called preperception. This is the matter of being in a situation. William James pointed out that somehow our perceptions depend on our being in a situation where we expect certain things. For example, when you are talking to somebody, you expect that particular person to say sounds of a particular language. In the current situation, I am speaking in English to you. That means there is a particular response habit node which is always strongly excited when I am in this situation. That node will give preperception influences into a lot of things which are then more ready to become excited than other things. These response habit nodes are where the subconscious comes in. You have response habit nodes for each situation in the past which you often don't think about. There are so many of them that you can't think about all of them. They are more or less ready to be thought about.

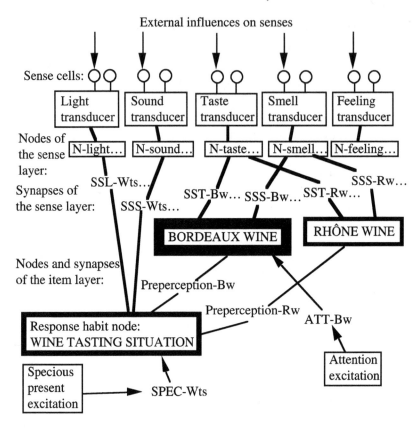

Figure 17.10: Perception and preperception [63, p.61].

Figure 17.11 is about imagination. Here you have impulses from
the node in the item layer going back to the nodes of the sense
layer. That gives visual imagery which is a very personal
thing; people are very different in this respect. Some have
strong visual imagery, others like me have very weak imagery.
It depends on these particular synapses (SS1, SS2, ...) and
whether they are conductive in this way or not, a well known
fact about psychology which James also discussed.

Figure 17.12 is part of a discussion about the response habit
node. For example, sitting here in this room at this moment,
I have sensations by light from a lot of things I see and they
combine into one particular response habit node which is my
being present in this room. At the same time, I can also

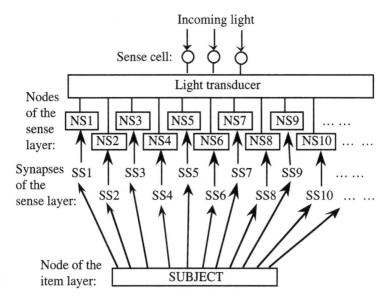

Figure 17.11: Experience of visual imagery [63, p.64].

have another node which more or less controls the kinds of things I speak. All in all, there will be five to ten response habit nodes strongly excited in each situation in which I find myself. That sort of selects from a lot of possible reactions those which actually come to the attention.

Table 17.1 is a summary of what James called the empirical life of Self — that is, personality. A person's Self is a matter of the person's habitual responses to certain sense impressions in certain situations. It is embodied in a certain number of response habit aggregates. For example, the desires to please and be noticed are controlled by response habit nodes.

Figure 17.13 shows the node aggregate for upright balance. How do you keep upright? That, again, is a matter of the synapses and how they have been trained.

Figure 17.14 shows an example of what I call a subject aggregate. This is the structure of nodes that are mostly in the item layer. When I am familiar with a subject, like Audrey Hepburn, then I know it by acquaintance. This means that if I am

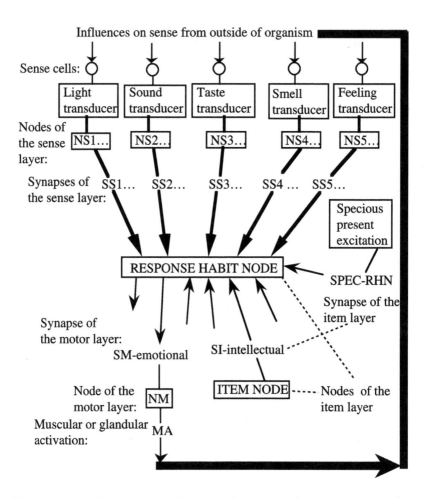

Figure 17.12: Excitations of node of response habit aggregate [63, p.70].

	MATERIAL	SOCIAL	SPIRITUAL
SELF-SEEKING	Bodily Appetites and Instincts Love of Adornment, Foppery, Acquisitiveness, Constructiveness, Love of Home, etc.	Desire to please, be noticed, admired, etc. Sociability, Emulation, Envy, Love, Pursuit of Honor, Ambition, etc.	Intellectual, Moral and Religious Aspiration, Conscientiousness
SELF-ESTIMA-TION	Personal Vanity, Modesty, etc. Pride of Wealth, Fear of Poverty	Social and Family Pride, Vainglory, Snobbery, Humility, Shame, etc.	Sense of Moral or Mental Superiority, Purity, etc. Sense of Inferiority or of Guilt

Table 17.1: James's summary of the empirical life of Self [63, p.75].

acquainted with Audrey Hepburn, then I have just one node in the item layer which belongs to Audrey Hepburn. That node is connected by conductive synapses to the fringe of Audrey Hepburn. The fringe contains other nodes such as the MOVIE FILM: WAR AND PIECE, the FICTIONAL CHARACTER: NATASHA who played in that movie, etc. All these nodes constitute the fringe; they will be weakly excited through the synapses. When my thinking goes round, my attention moves from one node to another. This is how the ordinary life of the stream of thought happens. When I see the letters that spell out the name "Audrey Hepburn", then I will sense these letters by light and, through conductive synapses SL-AH..., the node AUDREY HEPBURN will get excited. Likewise, if somebody speaks out the name "Audrey Hepburn", then I will sense by sound and, through conductive synapses SS-AH..., the node AUDREY HEPBURN will get excited. Or somebody would say to me: "Do you remember the actress who played the character Natasha in the movie War and Peace?" And then these two nodes — FICTIONAL CHARACTER: NATASHA and MOVIE FILM: WAR AND PIECE — would become excited and, in turn, through synapses SI-AH2 and SI-AH3 the node AUDREY

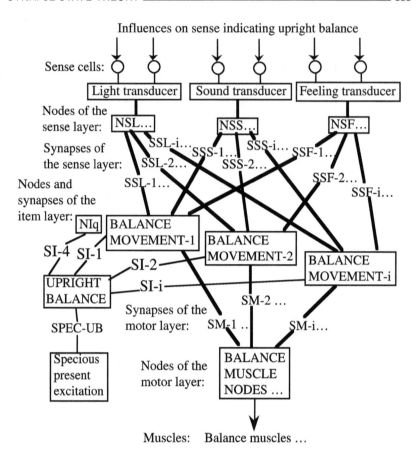

Figure 17.13: The node/synapse aggregate for upright balance [63, p.79].

HEPBURN will become excited too. In response, I would then say: "Yes I know her, but what was her name–..." In order to say her name, I have to activate the Action node say 'Audrey Hepburn'. Maybe I have it on my lips, or maybe I don't. This is a very common situation, which is a matter of one particular synapse, SI-sayAH, which connects the node AUDREY HEPBURN with the Action node say 'Audrey Hepburn'. That synapse will be strongly trained if I often speak her name. If, on the other hand, I don't often speak her name but only think of her, then that synapse will not be trained enough. In general, if you want to be able to talk

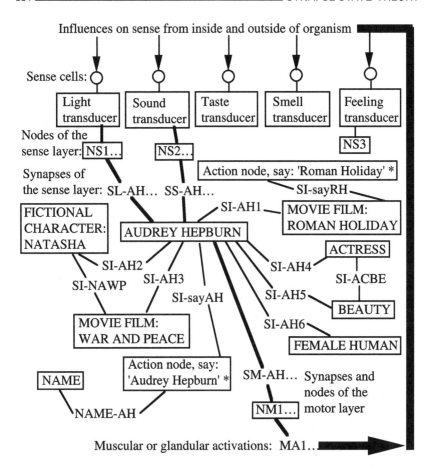

Figure 17.14: Subject aggregate: AUDREY HEPBURN [63, p.83].

about names of people, you should train them.

D: Yes, I noticed that reading books aloud seems to help. [N: Of course it does.]

Suppose Figure 17.14 resembles the activity that goes on in your brain when I speak out the words "Audrey Hepburn" at this very moment. If I understand you correctly, that figure will have to be modified in order to resemble your brain activity of the next time I speak out those very same words. That is, the picture is always changing. [N: That's right.] Now, you have stressed that memory is not a container. But, when I see these nodes in your figures, it makes me think of storage cells. So, to play the devil's advocate, why can I not view your theory by making an analogy with a computer?

N: The similarity of figures of computer structures and my figures of neural structures is merely a matter of the choice of certain graphical forms. The similarity does not extend to what these graphical forms are used to represent. In a picture of the structure of a computer, some of the boxes usually represent data stores (memories). Such data stores hold data, that is representations of what is being processed at any time. Some of the lines show transmission paths along which copies of the data are transferred among the stores. Other parts of the graph may show processors. Some of these control the traffic of data among the stores. Others represent processes by which data are converted. What is represented in my graphs of neural structures is quite different. There are no data stores, no representations that are held and transferred, and no processors. There are only three kinds of components: neurons, nodes, and synapses. The activity is merely a matter of excitations of various strengths of parts of the network of these components. Most of my figures show only a small part of the neural network and no excitations. Only Figures 17.7 and 17.10 also show the excitations, by the thickness of the frame drawn around some of the nodes. The excitations originate in the sense cells and the attention and specious present excitations sources. The overall pattern of excitations depends on the momentary conductivities of the synapses involved. In the short term, within seconds and minutes, the excitations of the nodes of the sense layer give rise to experience (the stream of thought), and those of the nodes of the motor layer give rise to activations of muscles and glands. In the long term (days and years) the excitations additionally give rise to plastic changes of the conductivities of the synapses connecting nodes that are sometimes excited at the same time, this being the mechanism of education of the nervous system. In some of the explanations the phrase 'the synapse(s)' for clarity should be expanded into 'the conductive synapse(s)'. Otherwise the

text may be misconstrued so as to say that synapses come
and go. They don't, they are there all the time, but most of
them are not conductive.

18. Neural impairments in a case of Alzheimer's disease

D: Let's discuss your 2009 paper 'Neural impairments in a case of Alzheimer's disease' [64]. Here you used your synapse-state theory to explain how Alzheimer happens in the nervous system.

N: I explained it on the basis of one particular case, the English author Iris Murdoch who suffered from Alzheimer starting from about 1984. Her illness has been described by her husband, John Bayley, and his description [3] is a unique introduction to how it actually happens. I have described the various symptoms observed by Bayley and how that may be understood. The symptoms are of different kinds. I found that I can explain all these symptoms by one single kind of defect developing in Murdoch's brain, to wit, the decay — one by one — of the nodes of her item layer. It was just that particular kind of component in her brain. It was not a matter of synapses or nodes of the sense layer or muscular layer. According to my description, these nodes in the item layer have, depending on the synapses, various functions. For instance, if you lose the subject node AUDREY HEPBURN, then you cannot think of Audrey Hepburn any more. But there are also other functions such as those of the response habit nodes. These nodes make you present in a situation. If you loose such a node, then you will, in a particular situation, not be able to recognize anything. That was very typical in the case of Iris Murdoch.

One of the first symptoms that Bayley described is a situation where he and his wife were together at a literature conference in Israel. As a writer of novels, Iris Murdoch had been invited to answer questions about her writings, something she had done many times before. At that particular conference in Israel, described by Bayley, the Question & Answer session was a complete failure. She could not speak at all. People asked questions and she didn't say anything, she didn't react at all. The chairman tried to mediate, but nothing helped. Half an hour later, she didn't know that it had been a failure. She hadn't registered that at all. I have explained all this by means of the response habit node which controlled her presence in a discussion session. Typically, in such a situation she would have a lot of preactivations of subject nodes related to her books, her characters, and the events she had written about. Thus, in a normal case, these subjects would have all been preactivated. But, if they are not preactivated, as was the case in Israel, then she could not perceive them at all, it made no sense to her, so she could not react to them. I have explained all this by one node. That was one symptom.

Later there were other symptoms. For example, Murdoch was, at some stage in her illness, not able to finish her phrases. Again, this can be explained by one particular node of the set of nodes which go into the speaking phrase. A phrase takes one syllable after the other, and each such syllable is activated by one node. But if one such node is inactive, then she will speak the first part of the phrase and no more. That is another typical symptom.

Everything in this Alzheimer case can be understood as the becoming inactive, one by one, of the nodes in the item layer.

D: Could you explain Figure 18.1 which is a figure from your paper?

N: This figure shows another problem Iris Murdoch had. She was writing her last novel about a character called Jackson. In this figure I show some of the nodes that had been in her mind when she had been planning to write the book. There was one node for the character Jackson and there was another

Nodes and synapses of the item layer

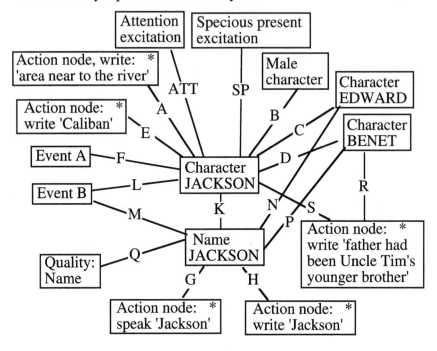

Figure 18.1: Iris Murdoch's loss of 'this man Jackson' [64, p.15].

node for the name Jackson, connected to action nodes so that she could speak it. Then, at a certain stage, this node 'Character JACKSON' disappeared. So all what she had been planning about how the character Jackson would appear in a number of situations in her novel suddenly dropped out.

D: Many thanks, Peter Naur, for this extensive discussion.

N: You are most welcome.

LONELY SCHOLAR™
SCIENTIFIC BOOKS

Don't miss our upcoming publications.
www.lonelyscholar.com

Conversations

The Future of Software Engineering: Panel Discussions
22–23 November 2010, ETH Zurich
scheduled release date: October 2011

Books

Dijkstra's Rallying Cry for Generalization
scheduled release date: early 2012

Bibliography

[1] J.W. Backus et al. "Report on the algorithmic language ALGOL 60". In: *Communications of the ACM* 3.5 (1960). Editor: P. Naur, pp. 299–314.

[2] J. Baragry. "Understanding Software Engineering: From Analogies With Other Disciplines To Philosophical Foundations". PhD thesis. Australia: La Trobe University, July 2000.

[3] J. Bayley. *Iris — A Memoir of Iris Murdoch.* 61 Frith Street, London, W1V 5TA: Gerald Duckworth & Co. Ltd., 1998.

[4] B.I. Blum. *Beyond Programming: To A New Era Of Design.* Oxford University Press, 1996.

[5] S. Chandrasekhar. *An Introduction to the Study of Stellar Structure.* University of Chicago Press, 1939.

[6] P.J. Denning. "A hard look at structured programming". In: *Structured Programming.* Maidenhead, England: Infotech State of the Art Report, 1976, pp. 183–202.

[7] E.W. Dijkstra. "A Constructive Approach to the Problem of Program Correctness". In: *BIT* 8 (1968), pp. 174–186.

[8] E.W. Dijkstra. *Notes on Structured Programming.* Tech. rep. T.H.-Report 70-WSK-03. Second edition. Technische Hogeschool Eindhoven, Apr. 1970.

[9] E.W. Dijkstra. "A position paper on software reliability". In: *Software Engineering Notes, ACM SIGSOFT.* Vol. 2. 5. Oct. 1977, pp. 3–5.

[10] E.W. Dijkstra. *Selected Writings on Computing: A Personal Perspective.* New York, Heidelberg, Berlin: Springer-Verlag, 1982.

[11] E.W. Dijkstra. *EWD 1000: Twenty-eight years.* Tech. rep. Jan. 1987.

[12] H.L. Dreyfus. *What Computers Can't Do: The Limits of Artificial Intelligence*. Revised edition (the first edition was in 1972). New York: Harper/Colophon, 1979.

[13] H.L. Dreyfus. *What Computers Still Can't Do: A Critique of Artificial Intelligence*. MIT Press, 1992.

[14] R.W. Floyd. "Assigning Meanings to Programs". In: *Proceedings of Symposia in Applied Mathematics*. Vol. 19. American Mathematical Society. 1967.

[15] *FM 2011: 17th International Symposium on Formal Methods, 20-24 June*. http://sites.lero.ie/fm2011/. 2011.

[16] G.H. Golub and L.B. Smith. "Algorithm 414, Chebyshev approximation of continued functions by a Chebyshev system of functions". In: *Communications of the ACM* 14 (1971), pp. 737–746.

[17] R. Goodman, ed. *Annual Review in Automatic Programming 4*. Pergamon Press, 1964.

[18] S. Gorn. "Specification Languages for Mechanical Languages and Their Processors — A Baker's Dozen". In: *Communications of the ACM* 4 (Dec. 1961), pp. 532–541.

[19] W. Henhapl and C.B. Jones. "A formal definition of ALGOL 60 as described in the 1975 Modified Report". In: *The Vienna development method: the meta-language*. Ed. by D. Bjørner and C.B. Jones. Lecture Notes in Computer Science 61. Berlin - Heidelberg - New York: Springer, 1978, pp. 305–336.

[20] R. Hyman and B. Anderson. "Solving Problems". In: *International Science and Technology* (Sept. 1965), pp. 36–41.

[21] W. James. *The Principles of Psychology, Vol. I-II*. Reprinted in Dover, 1950. Henry Holt, 1890.

[22] J. Jensen, P. Mondrup, and P. Naur. "A Storage Allocation Scheme for ALGOL 60". In: *Communications of the ACM* (1961), pp. 441–445.

[23] C.B. Jones. *Software Development: A Rigorous Approach*. Englewood Cliffs, New Jersey: Prentice-Hall, 1980.

[24] C.B. Jones. *Systematic Software Development Using VDM*. Englewood Cliffs, New Jersey: Prentice-Hall, 1986.

[25] D.E. Knuth. *The Art of Computer Programming, Vol. 1.* Reading, Massuchesettes: Addison-Wesley, 1968.

[26] H. Kreisler. *Meaning, Relevance, and the Limits of Technology — Conversation with Hubert L. Dreyfus.* Conversations with History. http://globetrotter.berkeley.edu/people5/Dreyfus/dreyfus-con0.html. Institute of International Studies, UC Berkeley, Nov. 2005.

[27] J. McCarthy. "Problems in the Theory of Computation". In: *IFIP Congress 65.* Vol. 1. 1965, pp. 219–222.

[28] J. McCarthy. "A Formal Description of a Subset of ALGOL". In: *Formal Language Description Languages for Computer Programming.* Ed. by T.B. Steel Jr. Conference was held in September 1964. North-Holland, 1966, pp. 1–7.

[29] D. Michie. *Machine Intelligence and Related Topics.* New York: Gordan and Breach, 1982.

[30] *Modern Computing Methods.* 2nd. Notes on Applied Science, No. 16. National Physical Laboratory, 1961.

[31] P. Naur. "The orbit of comet du Toit-Neujmin-Delporte (1941 e)". In: *Det kgl. Danske Videnskabernes Selskab, Mat. fys. Medd* 22.1 (1945).

[32] P. Naur. "Beretning om programstyrede elektronregnemaskiner i England, U.S.A. og Sverige (Report on programmed electronic computers in England, the U.S.A. and Sweden)". May 1954.

[33] P. Naur. "Elektronregnemaskinerne og hjernen (The electronic computer and the brain)". In: *Perspektiv* 1.7 (1954). Reprinted in [57, Sec. 8.1], pp. 42–46.

[34] P. Naur. "Albert Einstein (obituary)". In: *Nordisk astronomisk tidsskrift* 2 (1955), pp. 36–40.

[35] P. Naur. "The design of the Gier Algol Compiler". In: *BIT Nordisk Tidskrift for Informationsbehandling* 3 (1963). Reprinted in [17, p.49–85] and [57, Sec. 3.1]. Russian translation: Sovremennoye Programmirovanie, Sovjetskoye Radio, Moskva 1996, p. 161–207, pp. 124–140, 145–166.

[36] P. Naur. "Checking of Operand Types in Algol Compilers". In: *BIT Nordisk Tidskrift for Informationsbehandling* 5 (1965). Originally presented in NordSAM 64 Stockholm, August 1964. Reprinted in [57, Sec. 3.2], pp. 151–163.

[37] P. Naur. "The Place of Programming in a World of Problems, Tools, and People". In: *Proceedings IFIP Congress 65*. Reprinted in [57, Sec. 1.1]. 1965, pp. 195–199.

[38] P. Naur. "Proof of Algorithms by General Snapshots". In: *BIT Nordisk Tidskrift for Informationsbehandling* 6 (1966). Reprinted in [57, Sec. 5.2], pp. 310–316.

[39] P. Naur. "Successes and failures of the Algol effort". In: *Algol Bulletin* 28 (July 1968). Reprinted in [57, Sec. 2.2], pp. 58–62.

[40] P. Naur. "Programming by Action Clusters". In: *BIT Nordisk Tidskrift for Informationsbehandling* 9 (1969). Reprinted in [57, Sec. 5.3], pp. 250–258.

[41] P. Naur. "An experiment on program development". In: *BIT Nordisk Tidskrift for Informationsbehandling* 12.3 (1972). Reprinted in [57, Sec. 6.1], pp. 347–365.

[42] P. Naur. *Concise Survey of Computer Methods*. Chapter 1 reprinted in [57, Sec. 1.2]. Studentlitteratur, Lund, 1974.

[43] P. Naur. "Programming Languages, Natural Languages, and Mathematics". In: *Communications of the ACM* 18.12 (Dec. 1975). Reprinted in [57, Sec. 1.3], pp. 676–683.

[44] P. Naur. "Impressions of the early days of programming". In: *BIT Nordisk Tidskrift for Informationsbehandling* 20 (1980), pp. 414–425.

[45] P. Naur. "Aad van Wijngaarden's contribution to ALGOL 60". In: *Algorithmic Languages*. Ed. by de Bakker and van Vliet. Reprinted in [57, Sec. 2.3]. North-Holland, 1981, pp. 293–304.

[46] P. Naur. "An empirical approach to program analysis and construction". In: *Systems Architecture, Proceedings of the sixth ACM European regional conference, ICS 81*. ISBN 0-86103-050-8. Reprinted in [57, Sec. 6.2]. Westbury House, Guildford, Surrey, England, 1981, pp. 265–272.

[47] P. Naur. "Formalization in program development". In: *BIT Nordisk Tidskrift for Informationsbehandling* 22 (1982). Reprinted in [57, Sec. 7.1], pp. 437–453.

[48] P. Naur. "Review of E.W. Dijkstra: Selected writings on computing: a personal perspective". In: *Science of Computer Programming* 2.3 (Dec. 1982). Published August 1983, pp. 269–272.

[49] P. Naur. "Program development studies based on diaries". In: *Psychology of Computer Use*. Ed. by T.R.G. Green, S.J. Payne, and G.C. van der Veer. ISBN 0-12-297420-4. Reprinted in [57, Sec. 6.3]. London: Academic Press, 1983, pp. 159–170.

[50] P. Naur. "Intuition in software development". In: *Formal Methods and Software Development, Vol. 2: Colloquium on Software Engineering*. Ed. by H. Ehrig et al. Lecture Notes in Computer Science 186. ISBN 3-540-15199-0. Reprinted in [57, Sec. 7.2]. Berlin: Springer-Verlag, 1985, pp. 60–79.

[51] P. Naur. "Programming as theory building". In: *Microprocessing and Microprogramming* 15 (1985). Reprinted in [57, Sec. 1.4], pp. 253–261.

[52] P. Naur. "Review 8502-0062 of D. Michie: Machine intelligence and related topics". In: *Computing Reviews* 26.2 (Feb. 1985). Reprinted in [57, Sec. 8.3], pp. 101–104.

[53] P. Naur. "Thinking and Turing's Test". In: *BIT Nordisk Tidskrift for Informationsbehandling* 26 (1986). Reprinted in [57, Sec. 8.2], pp. 175–187.

[54] P. Naur. "Programmeringssprog er ikke sprog (Programming languages are not languages)". In: *Mal og Maele 2* 12 (1988). Gads Boghandel, Copenhagen. English version in [57, Sec. 8.4], pp. 24–31.

[55] P. Naur. "The place of strictly defined notation in human insight". In: *Workshop on Programming Logic, Bastad, Sweden*. Ed. by P. Dybjer et al. Reprinted in [57, Sec. 7.5]. Report 54, Programming Methodology Group, University of Göteborg and Chalmers University of Technology, Göteborg, Sweden, May 1989, pp. 429–443.

[56] P. Naur. "Computing and the so-called foundations of the so-called sciences". In: *Informatics Curricula for the 1990s*.

Invited lecture. Reprinted in [57, Sec. 1.5]. IFIP Wokring Group 3.2 Workshop. Providence, Rhode Island, Apr. 1990.

[57] P. Naur. *Computing: A Human Activity*. New York: ACM Press/Addison-Wesley, 1992.

[58] P. Naur. "Understanding Turing's Universal Machine—Personal Style in Program Description". In: *The Computer Journal* 36.4 (1993), pp. 351–372.

[59] P. Naur. *Knowing and the Mystique of Logic and Rules*. ISBN 0-7923-3680-1. Kluwer Academic Publishers, 1995, xii + 365 pages.

[60] P. Naur. *Antiphilosophical Dictionary: Thinking - Speech - Science/Scholarship*. ISBN 87-987221-1-5. naur.com publishing, 2001.

[61] P. Naur. *An anatomy of human mental life—Psychology in unideological reconstruction—incorporating the synapse-state theory of mental life*. www.naur.com/Nauranat-ref.html, ISBN 87-987221-3-1. naur.com publishing, Feb. 2005.

[62] P. Naur. "Computing versus human thinking, A.M. Turing Award Lecture". In: *Communications of the ACM* 50.1 (Jan. 2007), pp. 85–94.

[63] P. Naur. *The neural embodiment of mental life by the synapse-state theory*. ISBN 87-987221-5-8. naur.com publishing, 2008.

[64] P. Naur. "Neural impairments in a case of Alzheimer's disease". naur.com publishing. 2009.

[65] P. Naur. *Misapprehensions around 'knowledge'*. Invited lecture. Presented at the conference 'Click-on-knowledge 2011: Web-based knowledge and Contemporary Scholarship', Copenhagen. Available from http://www.naur.com/. May 2011.

[66] P. Naur and B. Randell, eds. *Software Engineering*. Reprinted in [67]. Report on a Conference sponsored by NATO Science Committee, held in 1968. Jan. 1969.

[67] P. Naur, B. Randell, and J.N. Buxton, eds. *Software Engineering: Concepts and Techniques*. New York: Petrocelli/Carter, 1976.

[68] K.R. Popper. *The logic of scientific discovery.* 10th impression, Hutchinson, 1980. London: Hutchinson, 1959.

[69] B. Randell, ed. *The Origins of Digital Computers: Selected Papers.* Springer-Verlag, 1973.

[70] *Report on the preparation of programmes for the EDSAC and the use of the library of subroutines.* Tech. rep. University Mathematical Laboratory Cambridge, Sept. 1950.

[71] B. Russell. *The Analysis of Mind.* London: George Allen & Unwin, 1921.

[72] B. Russell. *A History of Western Philosophy And Its Connection with Political and Social Circumstances from the Earliest Times to the Present Day.* New York: Simon and Schuster, 1945.

[73] B. Russell. "On the Notion of Cause". In: *Mysticism and Logic.* Originally published in 1912. London: Penguin, 1953, pp. 171–196.

[74] B. Russell. "Mathematics and metaphysicians". In: *Mysticism and Logic.* Originally published in 1901. Harmondsworth: Penguin, 1954, pp. 74–94.

[75] T.B. Steel, ed. *IFIP Working Conference on Formal Language Description Languages.* Amsterdam: North-Holland, 1966.

[76] A.M. Turing. "On Computable Numbers, with an Application to the Entscheidungsproblem". In: *Proceedings of the London Mathematical Society, 2nd series* 42 (1936), pp. 230–265.

[77] J. Watson. *The Double Helix.* New York: Signet, 1968.

[78] N. Wirth. "Program Development by Stepwise Refinement". In: *Communications of the ACM* 14 (Apr. 1971), pp. 221–227.

[79] N. Wirth. "On the Composition of Well-Structured Programs". In: *Computing Surveys* 6.4 (Dec. 1974), pp. 247–259.